Authors of Follett Social Studies

Janet E. Alleman-Brooks
Professor of Elementary Education:
 Social Studies
Department of Elementary
 and Special Education
Michigan State University
East Lansing, Michigan

Phillip Bacon
Professor of Geography
Department of Geography
University of Houston
Houston, Texas

Stephen S. Birdsall
Professor of Geography
Department of Geography
The University of North Carolina
 at Chapel Hill
Chapel Hill, North Carolina

JoAnne Buggey
Department of Elementary Education
University of Minnesota
Minneapolis, Minnesota

John Edwin Coffman
Associate Professor of Geography
Department of Geography
University of Houston
Houston, Texas

Donald C. Fairweather
Director of Curriculum and Instruction
Shepherd Independent School District
Shepherd, Texas

William W. Joyce
Professor of Education
Department of Elementary
 and Special Education
Michigan State University
East Lansing, Michigan

James B. Kracht
Associate Professor of Education
Department of Educational Curriculum
 and Instruction
Texas A&M University
College Station, Texas

Charles B. Myers
Professor of Social Studies Education
Department of Teaching and Learning
Peabody College of Vanderbilt University
Nashville, Tennessee

Arthur S. Nichols
Associate Professor of Elementary Education
Department of Elementary Education
California State University
Northridge, California

M. Evelyn Swartz
Professor of Elementary Education
School of Education
University of Kansas
Lawrence, Kansas

Gordon Wilk
Department Chairperson and Teacher:
 Social Studies
Carnegie Junior High School
Los Angeles Unified High School
Los Angeles, California

Follett Social Studies

Our United States

Annotated Teacher's Edition

Author
JoAnne Buggey

Follett Publishing Company
Chicago, Illinois

Atlanta, Georgia • Dallas, Texas
Sacramento, California • Warrensburg, Missouri

Table of Contents for Annotated Teacher's Edition

Page	
TE 4	Follett Social Studies—an Introduction
TE 12	Introducing *Our United States*
TE 14	Introducing the Annotated Teacher's Edition
TE 18	Teaching Map and Globe Skills
TE 20	Teaching Social Studies Reading Skills
TE 21	Teaching Thinking Skills
TE 22	Using Communication Skills
TE 22	Using Time Skills
TE 22	Using Math Skills
TE 23	Teaching Citizenship Skills
TE 24	Metric Conversion Table
TE 25	Answer Key for Text Questions

38   UNIT 1   AMERICA THE BEAUTIFUL
In the first unit the students examine the landscapes and people of the United States.

50   UNIT 2   THE FIRST AMERICANS
This unit examines the first Americans today and long ago, grouping the Indians according to the geographic areas in which they lived.

82   UNIT 3   EXPLORING THE NEW WORLD
This unit examines early explorers of the New World, focusing on Columbus as well as on early Spanish, English, French, and Dutch explorers.

114   UNIT 4   COLONIES IN NORTH AMERICA
This unit examines the Spanish, English, French, and Dutch colonies in North America, with a focus on the growth of the thirteen English colonies.

146   UNIT 5   CREATING A NEW NATION
This unit examines the years of transition from the thirteen British colonies to the new United States of America.

180   UNIT 6   LOOKING WESTWARD
This unit examines the new nation, focusing on settlement of the West and the industrial revolution.

214   UNIT 7   WAR AND A NEW BEGINNING
This unit examines the Civil War period—before, during, and after the war.

248   UNIT 8   A MODERN NATION
This unit examines the growth of the new nation.

Copyright © 1983 by Follett Publishing Company, a division of Follett Corporation. All rights reserved. No portion of this book may be reproduced in any form without written permission from the publisher. Manufactured in the United States of America.

Page

282 UNIT 9 THE UNITED STATES TODAY
This unit examines the United States from World War II to the present.

308 UNIT 10 THE NORTHEAST
This unit examines the Northeast, its population density, and its main types of employment.

326 UNIT 11 THE GREAT LAKES REGION
This unit examines the Great Lakes Region, its population density, and its main types of employment.

342 UNIT 12 THE MIDWEST PLAINS
This unit examines the Midwest Plains, its population density, and the major crops grown there.

358 UNIT 13 THE SOUTH
This unit examines the South, why its population is growing, and the major ways its people make a living.

376 UNIT 14 THE SOUTHWEST
This unit examines the Southwest, its population density, and the major ways its people make a living.

392 UNIT 15 THE INTERIOR WEST
This unit examines the Interior West, its population density, and the main occupations of the people who live there.

408 UNIT 16 THE PACIFIC COAST
This unit examines the Pacific Coast, its population density, and the main occupations of the people who live there.

424 UNIT 17 ALASKA AND HAWAII
This unit examines Alaska and Hawaii as a region, the region's population density, and the main occupations of the people who live there.

436 UNIT 18 CANADA
This unit examines Canada, how the geographies of Canada and the United States are alike yet different, how geography influences Canada's population patterns, and the major ways Canadians make a living.

452 UNIT 19 LATIN AMERICA
This unit examines Latin America, how the geographies of Latin America and the United States are different and alike, how geography influences Latin America's population patterns, and the major products of Latin America.

470 UNIT 20 THE UNITED STATES IN THE 21ST CENTURY
This unit examines the United States at the beginning of the 21st century, how predicted population patterns compare with those of the early 20th century, the importance of energy resources, and technological advances.

TE 3

Follett Social Studies—an Introduction

Kindergarten level	**My World** (full color work sheets)
Level one	**Home and School**
Level two	**People in Neighborhoods**
Level three	**Our Communities**
Level four	**World Regions**
Level five	**Our United States**
Level six/seven	**Latin America and Canada**
Level six/seven	**Our World Today**
Level six/seven	**People, Time, and Change**

Work Sheets—levels 1 and 2. Individual activities in duplicating master format that reinforce, extend, and evaluate content and skills presented in the textbook. Suggested teaching procedures included.

Workbooks—levels 3 through 6/7. Student booklets providing individual activities that review, reinforce, and enrich skills and content presented in the textbook. One workbook page for each chapter of the student text. Maps, graphs, and other illustrations included to reinforce social studies skills and engage student interest. Teacher's Editions provide answers to questions in student booklets.

Unit Tests—levels 3 through 6/7. Padded sets of evaluation exercises for each unit in the student text. Format based on principles of standardized testing. Teacher's answer key included.

Teacher's Activity Cards—Kindergarten level. Boxed set of cards presenting lesson plans and suggested teaching activities that encompass the kindergarten program. To be used in combination with student's padded full color work sheets.

Teacher's Resource Books—levels 1 through 6/7. Guided lesson plans, background information, application and extension activities, plus professional reference materials that aid teachers in planning and effecting an exceptional social studies program.

Program Overview

Follett Social Studies is a basal program designed to help students understand themselves and others in the world around them. Its content stems from the facts, concepts, and skills that have formed the cornerstones of elementary social studies for more than forty years. The structured components of this easy-to-teach program safeguard the dual objectives of content and process that make social studies a rewarding experience for both students and teachers.

Content

Throughout the series the focus is on an interdisciplinary approach. Although particular emphasis is given to geography and history—especially in the upper grades—political science, economics, sociology, and anthropology are also stressed (see pages TE 8–9). A selected number of basic concepts from each of the social sciences have been identified (see pages TE 10–11). These concepts are an important element of the Follett Social Studies program. When appropriate, the humanities have been focused on. An expanding horizons approach has been used to select relevant content with a focus on the real world. Realistic roles, as suggested by the National Council for the Social Studies, are also examined throughout the program. The interrelationship of concepts, content, and roles is diagramed on page TE 7.

Skills

Follett Social Studies is a skills-building program. It is organized around skills that can turn young students into lifelong learners. Students are introduced to and given opportunities to use a variety of skills. These include map and globe skills, reading skills, thinking skills, communication skills, time skills, math skills, and citizenship skills. Stress is on application and reinforcement of skills throughout the program. Subsequent pages of the Annotated Teacher's Edition describe these important skills areas.

Photographs, maps, charts, graphs, and other illustrative materials are used whenever appropriate to aid understanding of the text by providing concrete images. A variety of writing styles and special features provide change of pace and heightened motivation. A carefully controlled reading level (at or below grade level) has been considered in each book.

Citizenship

Throughout Follett Social Studies, students are given opportunities to understand the importance of attitudes and beliefs—their own, those of other individuals and groups, and those of society in general. Particular attention is paid to skills. The methods employed allow meaningful exploration that will promote greater understanding and preparation for life as participating citizens. Both the school and the community are used as learning environments. Particular emphasis is devoted to the democratic values that are an important part of our American heritage.

Today and the Future

Most students in today's elementary classrooms will spend more than half of their lives in the 21st century. As educators, we must prepare these students not only for today's world but also for tomorrow's. As a result, our role in a globally interdependent world is examined. The ever changing world of work is also explored. Human knowledge will continue to grow and change in the years ahead. Follett Social Studies will help students acquire a body of basic knowledge that will stand the test of time and provide a base upon which they can build skills for living in a changing world.

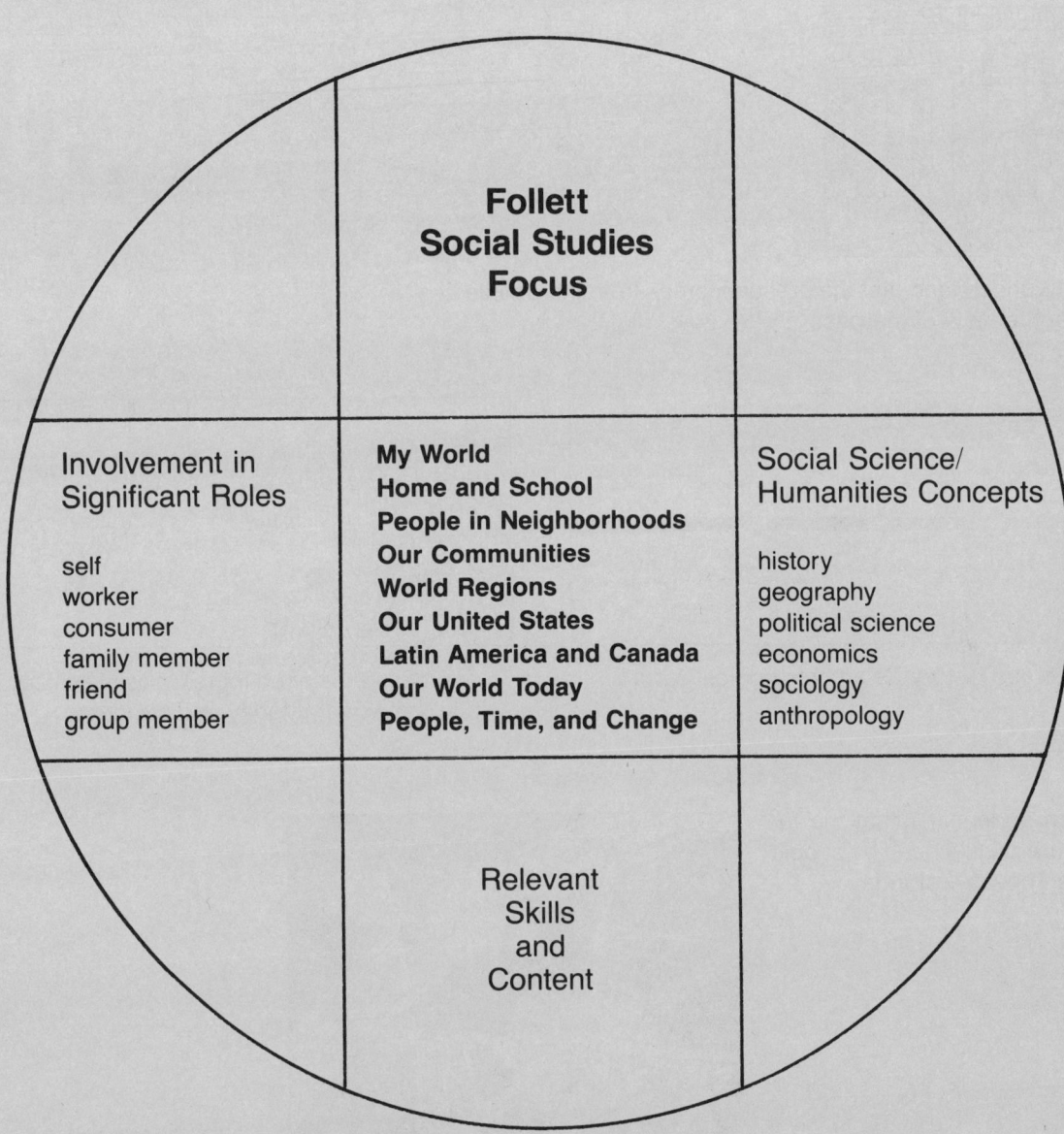

TE 7

The Basic Purpose of the Social Studies

To help children understand their physical and human world so that they may become better citizens.

Some major objectives that contribute to the basic purpose of the social studies:

History

 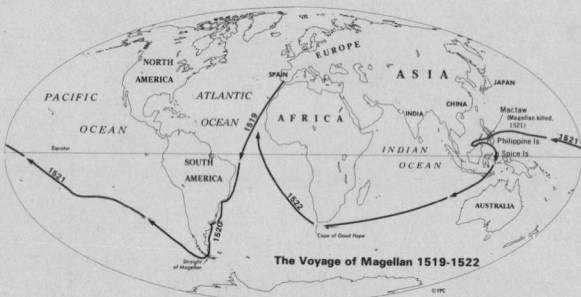 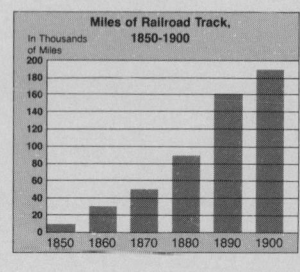

To understand that the present comes from the people and events of the past.

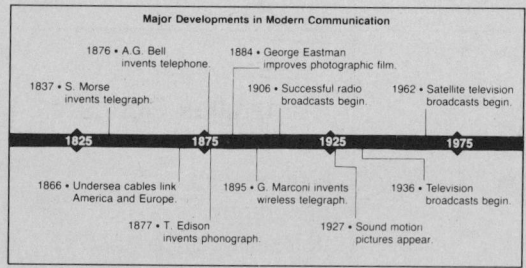

To see history as a chronological record.

To appreciate the need for responsible citizenship in the world of today and tomorrow.

To understand that the future is influenced by people and events of today.

TE 8

Geography and Economics

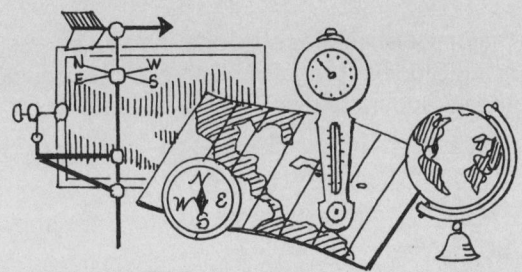

To become familiar with the tools and methods of geography.

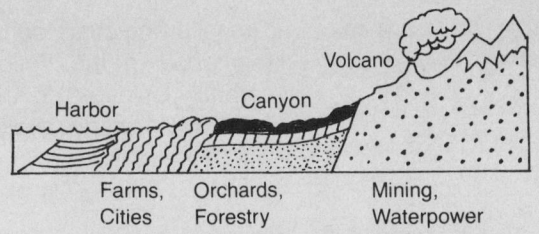

To learn the basic facts about our physical world and to understand human occupations in their geographical settings.

To recognize likenesses and differences in ways of living in different regions.

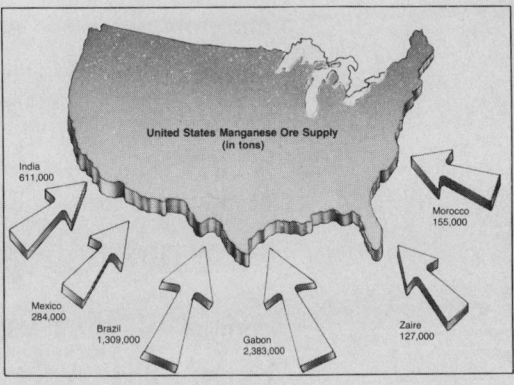

To recognize growing interdependence among people and nations.

Political Science, Sociology, and Anthropology

To understand the American system of government and to value its institutions.

To appreciate universal human qualities and understand cultural likenesses and differences among human groups.

To identify basic social institutions and some of their functions.

TE 9

Follett Social Studies Concepts

The following chart identifies major social studies concepts introduced and reinforced in the Follett Social Studies program. Content has been carefully selected to promote an understanding of these concepts at appropriate grade levels.

adaptation	Adjustment to natural or cultural environment.
change	Basic alterations in general attitudes, ways of life, patterns of living, technology, etc.
choice	Power or chance to choose or make a decision.
chronology	An arrangement of events in order of occurrence.
citizenship	The rights and responsibilities of members of a community or nation.
climate	Regional weather patterns.
communication	Exchange of information and ideas.
community	A group of people linked together by a common economic or political system.
conflict	Strong disagreement among individuals or groups.
conservation	Protection from being used up.
consume	To use.
cooperation	Working together to achieve a goal.
culture	Patterns of behavior.
democracy	System of government in which power is vested in the people.
diversity	Differences; variety.
environment	The social and physical world.
freedom	Opportunity to make choices within an established structure.
goods	Material things used to satisfy needs or wants.
government	An established system of rules and authority.
group	A number of people who interact, communicate, and share common interests and goals.
institutions	Established practices, relationships, or organizations in a culture or group.

interaction	Communication, conflict, or cooperation among individuals or groups.
interdependence	Reliance upon the exchange among nations, groups, or individuals.
justice	The fair treatment of all.
land use	Ways of utilizing the earth's resources.
leadership	The direction of a group of people in the achievement of a goal.
nation	A political region with a single central government.
needs	Things people must have for survival.
power	Control, authority, or influence.
produce	To grow, raise, make, or supply.
region	A major geographical area having at least one distinguishing feature.
resources	Things people use to meet their needs and wants.
responsibilities	Obligations accompanying membership in a group.
rights	Powers and privileges to which one is entitled.
roles	Patterns of behavior followed by people as they carry out particular functions.
rules	Guidelines for behavior.
scarcity	Limitation in availability of goods or services.
services	Work or activities performed to satisfy needs and wants.
society	A group of people sharing many common interests, beliefs, and attitudes.
technology	The means through which people supply their needs and wants by the use of tools.
trade	Exchange; buying, selling, or barter.
transportation	The means of moving goods and people from one place to another.
values	Standards, principles, and beliefs that influence behavior.
wants	Things people wish they could have.
work	What people do to meet their needs and wants.

Introducing *Our United States*

Our United States begins by introducing the Atlas included in the beginning of the text. The twenty units of the text expand student understandings of the United States and the other countries of the Western Hemisphere. The text is divided into two parts. The nine units in Part One present the history of the United States chronologically. Time lines are on the opening pages of each unit to help establish the time period included in the unit. Present-day regional studies are the focus of most of the units in Part Two. The tenth through the sixteenth units examine U.S. regions: the Northeast, the Great Lakes Region, the Midwest Plains, the South, the Southwest, the Interior West, and the Pacific Coast. The seventeenth unit focuses on the states of Alaska and Hawaii. The eighteenth and nineteenth units introduce Canada and Latin America. The final unit explores the 21st century.

Basic Goals

The basic goals of Follett Social Studies:

To help students understand themselves and others

To develop an understanding of concepts that are basic to social studies

To help students develop social studies skills needed in a changing world

To help students develop critical thinking skills

To encourage in students attitudes and behavior relevant to responsible citizenship

To make students aware of some of the many career choices that are part of the adult world and to develop positive attitudes toward the world of work

Basic Skills

The skills program is an integral part of the student text. Numerous opportunities are provided for the development of a wide variety of skills in many different contexts. The following basic skills are stressed throughout.

Map and Globe Skills. One of the major emphases of Follett Social Studies is the step-by-step development of the skills needed to use maps and globes. At each succeeding level the skills developed in previous books are extended and applied, and new skills are introduced. A collection of maps that will be useful for reference throughout the study of all units appears in the Atlas at the beginning of the text (see student pages 9–25). An illustrated Dictionary of Geographical Terms is also included (see student pages 26–27). The opening yellow-tinted section of the text, entitled The Atlas Tells a Story, introduces a number of map and globe skills (see student pages 28–35). Additional map and globe skills are introduced in subsequent yellow-tinted pages appearing within individual units of the text. These skills are extended and applied throughout the program. See pages TE 18–19 for the scope and sequence of map and globe skills.

Social Studies Reading Skills. The application of reading skills to social studies content enables students to develop reading skills as they master content (see page TE 20). The structure of the student text provides consistent development and application of content reading skills.

An As You Read box precedes each chapter of the text (see student page 65).

Item 1 of As You Read lists the social

As You Read
1. Think about these words.
   adobe   irrigate   hogan
2. Look for answers to these key questions.
   a. Where did the Pueblo and Navajo people live?
   b. Why did the Pueblo Indians irrigate their farms?
   c. In what ways did the Navajo change after they migrated to the Southwest?
3. Use this reading skill.
   Each chapter in this book begins with a list of important social studies words. You will also find these words in bold type as you read the chapters. The Glossary at the back of your book tells you how to pronounce these words and what they mean. Be sure you can pronounce each word and understand its meaning.

TE 12

studies–related vocabulary to be introduced. The teacher may read, pronounce, and/or have students study the Glossary definitions of these words before they read the text. These words are in boldface where they first appear in the text, and a definition is provided within the context of the material. Pronunciation is also included in the text when appropriate (see student page 56). Item 2 of As You Read provides the key questions to be focused on in that chapter of the text. These questions can be used to preview what is to come and to review and evaluate informally each chapter. Item 3 of As You Read appears as appropriate and introduces a particular reading skill to be stressed in that chapter.

Each Unit Review Workshop also includes exercises that reinforce content reading skills (see Use Your Reading Skills on student pages 112 and 144).

The vocabulary level of the student text has been carefully controlled. Short reading sections have been planned to present the carefully sequenced content. Lessons introduce new materials and reinforce and extend the materials developed in previous lessons. Questions are included within the text whenever appropriate. Students will be reinforcing their social studies reading skills throughout each unit.

Students learn to use books as reference tools by beginning with their own text—using the Table of Contents, Glossary, Index, headings, graphics, etc.—as appropriate. In addition, they have opportunities to do research in supplemental books and encyclopedias. Activities also give practice in organizing information for oral and written reports.

Thinking Skills. The ability to relate facts and work with ideas is essential to the intelligent practice of citizenship in a democracy. Cognitive development is necessary not only in the social studies but also in all areas of life. The development of basic thinking skills is a major emphasis throughout the text (see page TE 21 and student page 324). The final and italicized question of every Checking Up, which reviews chapter content, stresses higher-level thinking skills (see student page 155).

> Reading and thinking skills are so closely interwoven as to be almost inseparable; each involves the other. Although they are presented as discrete skills in the listings, it is important to remember the overlap and interweaving that exist.

Communication Skills. These include meaningful practice in listening, writing, and speaking. These skills are often an integral part of each lesson. They are also reinforced when appropriate in end-of-unit activities (see student page 112).

Time Skills. Whenever appropriate, time skills are reinforced within the text (see student page 212). The sidebar section Then and Now also fosters the understanding of time (see student page 202).

Math Skills. Social studies math skills are reinforced throughout the text (see student page 374). These skills have been selected to reinforce math skills presented in most basal math programs.

Citizenship Skills. Decision making and social participation are incorporated into the student materials (see Use Your Group Skills, student page 246). Three sidebar articles also stress citizenship skills. These are People Who Made a Difference, Careers, and Citizenship (see student pages 71, 419, 139).

Evaluation

Evaluation is an ongoing part of each level of the Follett Social Studies program. Opportunities for formal and informal evaluation are provided throughout the text. Checking Up questions appear at the end of each chapter (see student page 43). These questions are mainly for review. At the end of each unit, a two-page Review Workshop is included. Each Review Workshop provides opportunities to evaluate the facts, skills, and key ideas of the unit (see student pages 340, 341).

Introducing the Annotated Teacher's Edition

The Annotated Teacher's Edition opens with a section of buff-tinted pages that introduce the Follett Social Studies program and the student text. This section concludes with a teacher's Answer Key that gives answers for formal chapter questions and Unit Review Workshop activities in the student text.

The remainder of the Annotated Teacher's Edition has been carefully organized to provide suggestions for teaching each unit of the student text. Annotations overprinted in red on the student pages provide specific teaching suggestions for each unit and chapter.

On the first page of each two-page unit opener, annotations to guide the planning and teaching of each unit are presented (see page TE 15).

Unit Overview—A general statement of the focus of each unit.

Unit Objectives—Broadly stated objectives for each unit.

Skills Emphasized—List of skills specifically stressed in the unit introduction, in annotations on the student text pages of each unit, and in the Unit Review Workshop.

Suggested Materials—A list of other materials directly related to the unit.

Suggested Student Activities—A list of selected activities that could help to focus the study of each unit. Most activities suggested in the annotations are for use with all students; however, others have been suggested for students with different ability levels (see Individualizing Instruction on this page). *Skills Emphasized in Suggested Student Activities* are the skills stressed in the Suggested Student Activities.

Annotations overprinted in red on the student text pages of each unit have been selected to provide the following information:
- the specific reading skill focused on in As You Read, 3 (see student page 116)
- background information for the teacher (see student page 368)
- skills to be emphasized (see student pages 429, 431, and 434)
- additional opportunities for skill and concept development (see student page 444)
- related activities for the total class (see student page 55)
- related activities for individualizing instruction (see student pages 60, 65, and 68)
- answers to questions within the text (see student page 75)
- pronunciation of words or terms not pronounced in the text (see student page 61)
- suggestions to add to or extend sidebar readings (see student page 123)
- suggestions to extend or apply map and globe or graph skills on yellow-tinted pages (see student page 127)

Individualizing Instruction

Many of the activities in the Annotated Teacher's Edition are keyed to different ability levels of learners. Low-achieving students will have most success in completing activities designated with one asterisk (*). Two asterisks (**) indicate activities for average students. Three asterisks (***) indicate activities that will challenge students with high ability. Activities with no asterisk designation are appropriate for students of all ability levels.

A Unit at a Glance

- Unit Opener
- Chapter Title
- As You Read
- Text
- Checking Up
- Unit Summary
- Unit Review Workshop

Unit Overview: This unit examines the landscapes and people in the United States.

Unit Objectives
To understand:
- the major landforms in the United States
- the beliefs and spirit of the American people

Suggested Materials
Workbook
Unit Tests

Unit 1

Skills Emphasized
Map Skill: p. 43.
Social Studies Reading Skills: pp. 38, 40, 42, 43, 45, 48, 49.
Thinking Skills: pp. 38, 41, 45, 47, 48, 49.
Communication Skills: pp. 38, 47, 48.
Social Studies Math Skill: p. 44.
Citizenship Skill: p. 38.

Suggested Student Activities
1. Arrange a bulletin-board mural called "America the Beautiful."
2. Work in pairs. Make posters illustrating our freedoms.
3. List ways in which Americans are alike and different.
* 4. Divide a sheet into four sections. Illustrate the four basic landforms in the United States.
** 5. List examples of the kinds of work people do.
*** 6. Illustrate "America the Beautiful."

Skills Emphasized in Suggested Student Activities
Social Studies Reading Skills: Using references, doing research, organizing information.
Thinking Skills: Knowing, comparing, classifying.
Communication Skill: Writing.
Citizenship Skill: Social participation.

America the Beautiful

A river trip through the Grand Canyon would take one almost a mile in the depths of the earth.

Teaching a Unit

A two-page unit opener is a special feature throughout the student text (see student pages 32–33). When a new unit is introduced to students, the full-page photograph on the unit opener should be examined as an overview of the unit content. Students may observe details in the photograph that seem to relate to the title of the unit. Teachers will use the annotations printed in red on the first page of the unit opener for organizing and teaching the unit (see also Suggested Time Allotment on these pages).

A blue-tinted As You Read focus box precedes the text for each unit in levels one and two and each chapter of the other texts of the Follett Social Studies. The material in each blue-tinted box provides an introduction to the specific content of the lesson or lessons that follow. New vocabulary words should be studied for pronunciation and meaning before students begin reading. The key questions in the focus box should also be fixed in the students' minds as they begin to read the text. Students will read specifically to find answers to the key questions.

When relevant, the blue focus box also describes a reading skill to be stressed as students study the text. (An annotation above the focus box in the Annotated Teacher's Edition identifies the specific reading skill.) As the lesson is reviewed and discussed in class, the teacher may ask students to describe how they applied this reading skill and how they will reuse the skill to help them improve their reading proficiency in subsequent assignments.

The text's reading sections themselves are carefully controlled for length: each segment is compatible with student comprehension level and attention span. Graphics—photographs, maps, charts, graphs, diagrams—are a key part of the student text. Each has a definite purpose and should be examined carefully. Questions are included within the reading text when appropriate to the content. Often these questions refer students to graphics on the page or to maps in the Atlas. Consistent answering of these questions will not only ensure students' comprehension of important content concepts but also improve their reading skills. For the teacher's convenience, answers to many of the in-text questions have been provided in on-page annotations.

Teachers will also want to refer to the on-page annotations within student text reading sections for additional topics for class discussion, notes for handling specific points of information covered in the student text, and additional reinforcement activities that will motivate students.

In assigning student text readings, teachers will want to call attention to the sidebar articles set off in boxes outlined in red. Every text in Follett Social Studies includes the following special sidebar selections: Then and Now, readings that relate people and events of the past with present-day counterparts; Careers, readings that focus attention on the world of work and/or possible career opportunities; People Who Made a Difference, biographical sketches of persons or groups who have made positive contributions to society; and Citizenship, descriptions of ways in which people actively participate in building a better society. Reading and discussing these sidebar selections increase student insights and help to personalize the content of the text.

Every historical unit of the student text also includes one or more yellow-tinted pages on which geographical skills are introduced, applied, and/or extended (see student pages 191–194). The reading and interpretation of maps, graphs, diagrams, and other graphics receive special emphasis on these skills pages. The running text on these pages often directs students to the graphics to find specific information.

Frequent opportunities for formal review and evaluation are included in the student text. Beginning at level three of Follett Social Studies, each chapter concludes with a set of Checking Up questions. These questions review the essential facts of the chapter, including those highlighted in the key questions in the As You Read box, and provide a final question that asks students to *apply* information they have learned. Also beginning at level three, a list of statements recalling key data from the unit makes up a concluding Unit Summary. On-page annotations provide suggestions for use of this summary as a class activity (see student page 111).

A two-page Review Workshop concludes every unit. Under the first heading—What Have You Learned?—is a list of questions covering factual information from the unit. These questions in particular test student comprehension and recall of important content. Use Your Reading Skills, always the second set of activities in the Review Workshop, not only reviews content but also applies and reinforces specific reading skills. The remainder of the questions and activities on the Review Workshop pages develop skills selected from the other skills areas, including library skills, stressed in the Follett Social Studies program.

Groups and Grouping

Follett Social Studies is organized to provide students many opportunities to work cooperatively in groups of varied sizes. Suggestions for large group and small group interaction are presented in all texts. Group size should be varied to meet student needs and abilities.

Students with special needs should be incorporated into the daily social studies program. Students who are mainstreamed, those who have special language needs, and gifted students should all be active participants.

Follett Supplementary Materials

The following materials are available from Follett Publishing Company. See page TE 5 for descriptions of content and use.

Work Sheets—duplicating masters for levels 1 and 2.
Workbooks—for levels 3 through 6/7.
Unit Tests—for levels 3 through 6/7.
Teacher's Resource Books—for levels 1 through 6/7.

Suggested Time Allotment
The following suggested schedule will help the teacher plan the amount of time to devote to each unit of this book. Adjustments should be made to meet the needs of each class.

Atlas	2 weeks
Unit 1	1 week
Unit 2	2 weeks
Unit 3	2 weeks
Unit 4	2 weeks
Unit 5	2 weeks
Unit 6	2 weeks
Unit 7	1½ weeks
Unit 8	2 weeks
Unit 9	1½ weeks
Unit 10	1½ weeks
Unit 11	1½ weeks
Unit 12	1½ weeks
Unit 13	1½ weeks
Unit 14	1½ weeks
Unit 15	1½ weeks
Unit 16	1½ weeks
Unit 17	1 week
Unit 18	1 week
Unit 19	1 week
Unit 20	½ week

Sources of Related Materials

National Council for the Social Studies
3615 Wisconsin Avenue, N.W.
Washington, D.C. 20016

Social Studies School Service
10,000 Culver Boulevard
P.O. Box 802
Culver City, California 90230

Encyclopaedia Britannica Films
425 North Michigan Avenue
Chicago, Illinois 60611

McGraw-Hill, Text-Film Division
330 West 42nd Street
New York, New York 10036

National Aeronautics and Space Administration (NASA)
Washington, D.C. 20546

National Geographic Society
Department 76
P.O. Box 1640
Washington, D.C. 20013

Teaching Map and Globe Skills

The ability to understand and use maps and globes is essential to the study of the social sciences and useful throughout life. Map and globe study is introduced in kindergarten and developed throughout the Follett Social Studies program with a carefully sequenced presentation of skills and understandings focusing on location, scale, distance, symbolization, and projection.

Each level of the program includes a wide variety of map and globe representations as appropriate to the level and the content of the program. Each book begins with the Atlas, the Dictionary of Geographical Terms, and The Atlas Tells a Story—the first group of lessons the students study. Specially color-coded (yellow) pages focus on maps, globes, and other geographical skills and understandings throughout each text. Further attention is given to map and globe skills in the annotations at the beginning of each unit in the Annotated Teacher's Edition.

The scope and sequence chart on these pages indicates the major map and globe skills introduced, extended, and applied throughout the Follett Social Studies program.

Map and Globe Skills

○ Introduced ● Extended ■ Applied

	K	1	2	3	4	5	6/7
Location: Where is it?							
Using verbal directions	○	●	●	■	■	■	■
Relating location on a globe to location on earth	○	●	●	●	■	■	■
Understanding a grid system				○	●	■	■
Understanding cardinal directions				○	●	■	■
Using cardinal directions on a grid system				○	●	■	■
Using cardinal directions to locate places on maps				○	●	■	■
Understanding the equator				○	●	■	■
Understanding intermediate directions					○	●	■	■
Recognizing the Northern and Southern Hemispheres					○	●	■	■
Understanding parallels of latitude						○	●	■
Understanding the Eastern and Western Hemispheres							○	■
Understanding longitude							○	■
Understanding the global grid							○	●
Using longitude and latitude							○	■
Using the International Date Line to understand time zones								○

	K	1	2	3	4	5	6/7
Scale: How big is it?							
Using something small to represent something large	○	●	●	●	■	■	■
Understanding that maps are smaller than reality	○	●	●	■	■	■	■
Recognizing that the earth is too big to be seen all at once				○	●	■	■
Seeing that areas can be shown larger or smaller				○	●	■	■
Examining how scale and area are related				○	●	●	■
Interpreting a map scale					○	●	■
Distance: How far is it?							
Measuring distances			○	●	●	■	■
Relating distance to scale				○	●	■	■
Measuring distance on a globe					○	●	■
Using latitude and longitude to measure distance						○	■
Symbolization: What is it?							
Using color to represent things	○	●	●	●	■	■	■
Understanding symbols	○	●	●	■	■	■	■
Using pictorial and abstract symbols		○	●	●	■	■	■
Using a key or legend		○	●	●	■	■	■
Using thematic maps				○	●	■	■
Projection: How can a round surface be transferred to a flat surface?							
Examining the globe	○	●	●	●	■	■	■
Understanding maps	○	●	●	■	■	■	■
Comparing a map and a globe	○	●	●	■	■	■	■
Examining kinds of maps				○	●	●	■
Comparing projections					○	●	■
Making a map from a globe						○	●

TE 19

Teaching Social Studies Reading Skills

Social studies teachers and texts do not teach reading per se. Yet if students are to be successful in mastering social studies content, they must master a variety of content reading skills. The Follett Social Studies program aims at six major reading proficiency goals that can be attained through the use of the program. These goals and the specific content reading skills associated with them are shown in the chart below. They are reinforced throughout the Follett Social Studies program as appropriate to the content and where normally introduced in a basal reading series. For example, an Appendix is included in the program beginning with level five.

Teachers will find ample help in working toward these goals in both the texts and the Annotated Teacher's Editions. Each unit readiness page for levels one and two and each chapter opening for levels three and up includes an As You Read section that introduces new social studies vocabulary and helps focus student reading skills throughout the unit. All texts include unit-ending exercises that provide further practice in the use of reading skills. Whenever appropriate, additional suggestions are contained in the unit introductions and annotations in the Annotated Teacher's Edition.

SOCIAL STUDIES READING SKILLS

ENRICHING VOCABULARY
Building social studies vocabulary
Determining meaning from context

COMPREHENSION
Previewing a reading selection
Skimming for information
Recognizing main ideas
Seeing relationships
Recognizing time order
Identifying point of view
Discovering cause and effect
Recognizing the author's purpose
Reading for details
Using details to support main ideas
Interpreting facts
Distinguishing fact from opinion
Distinguishing fact from fantasy
Drawing conclusions
Paraphrasing
Following directions

ORGANIZING INFORMATION
Alphabetizing
Note taking
Outlining
Listing
Summarizing
Constructing charts, graphs, time lines, etc.

INTERPRETING GRAPHICS
Maps
Photographs and illustrations
Graphs
Charts
Forms
Diagrams
Tables
Captions
Cartoons
Symbols and signs
Satellite imagery

USING TEXTBOOK FEATURES
Headings
Table of Contents
Atlas
Appendix
Glossary
Index
Title Page
Sidebar readings

USING REFERENCE TOOLS/ DOING RESEARCH
Newspapers and magazines
Dictionaries
Encyclopedias
Almanacs
Globes
Libraries

Teaching Thinking Skills

Useful thinking skills grow naturally from the social sciences. There is a mass of facts concerning the world we live in. These facts must be put to use in a meaningful way.

Teaching thinking skills is made easier by the innate curiosity of the young. The first step in teaching thinking skills is to engage that curiosity. The second is to enlarge it. And the third is to direct it with sound methodology. For students to gain knowledge systematically and to make decisions based on reliable data, they must become questioners as well as receivers of facts and interpretations. In the social studies it is important to arrange situations, activities, and opportunities for independent thinking on the part of students.

Follett Social Studies introduces thinking skills at the kindergarten level and builds upon them at each succeeding level. Effective questioning is at the core of thinking skills development. The text material at each level uses questions to promote the development of thinking skills and to encourage their application to problem-solving situations.

Thinking skills activities are built into each student text. They can be found within each unit and in the unit-ending activities of the Review Workshop pages. The Annotated Teacher's Edition suggests activities on the first page of each unit and in the annotations on the student pages. To help students develop into thoughtful, reasoning citizens and to help them develop productive and open outlooks on life are among the most important goals of the social studies. The following basic thinking skills are stressed in the Follett Social Studies program.

THINKING SKILLS

Knowing	Analyzing
Observing	Synthesizing
Classifying	Predicting
Comparing	Hypothesizing
Generalizing/Inferring	Evaluating

Using Communication Skills

Follett Social Studies reinforces the communication skills of listening, writing, and speaking. Listening skills include—
- gathering information
- following directions
- answering questions
- responding to nonverbal clues.

Writing skills include—
- composing original materials
- organizing reports
- using forms
- keeping records.

Speaking skills include—
- contributing to discussions
- asking and answering questions
- working in groups
- using skills
- giving directions.

Opportunities to use these skills are provided when appropriate to the content and the abilities of the students. Listening, writing, and speaking may be a part of each lesson. Annotations on the opening page of each unit and on selected student pages identify where these skills are specifically reinforced.

Communication Skills
Listening skills
Writing skills
Speaking skills

Using Time Skills

Time skills are an important part of the Follett Social Studies program. At each level students have an opportunity to expand their understanding of the past, present, and future. Time skills include—
- building time-related vocabulary
- using calendars, clocks, etc.
- sequencing events
- examining time relationships.

A sidebar section, Then and Now, is included to emphasize time skills at each level of the program.

Time skills are reinforced in each student text and in unit-ending activities when relevant. Additional suggestions can be found throughout the Teacher's Annotated Edition.

Using Math Skills

Math skills are reinforced throughout the Follett Social Studies program. Skills related to the content and appropriate to learner abilities are suggested. Activities were selected at each grade level based upon skills taught in most basal math programs. Math skills include opportunities to—
- read and write numbers
- estimate
- compute
- solve word problems
- measure
- use statistics.

Whenever appropriate, students are asked to apply math skills to everyday situations. Opportunities are provided to read, interpret, and construct tables, graphs, and charts. The place of the computer in today's world has also been considered. Math skills are reinforced in the student text and in the unit-ending activities when relevant. Additional suggestions can be found throughout the Annotated Teacher's Edition.

Teaching Citizenship Skills

Citizenship skills are an integral part of the Follett Social Studies program at all levels. They are an informal part of every lesson and are stressed when appropriate to the content throughout each text.

Decision making is a major focus of the program. Students are continuously—
- identifying choices
- considering alternatives
- considering the consequences of the alternatives
- making decisions
- following through once decisions are made.

Often these skills are used informally in daily lessons. At other times these decision-making skills are the focus of specific lessons.

The Follett Social Studies program also stresses social participation skills. Throughout the program students are asked to—
- consider self and others
- work in groups
- accept responsibilities
- receive feedback
- examine stereotypes
- utilize community resources.

Whenever appropriate, materials should be related directly to your own students and their community.

Opportunities for discussing, identifying, and clarifying these citizenship skills are presented in the unit-ending activities and within the body of the student text. Suggestions can also be found throughout the pages of the Annotated Teacher's Edition.

Citizenship Skills
Decision making
Social participation

Metric Conversion Table

Converting Standard Measurement to Metric Measurement

	To convert:	**Into:**	**Multiply by:**
Length	inches (in.)	millimeters (mm)	25.4
	inches	centimeters (cm)	2.54
	feet (ft.)	centimeters	30.5
	feet	meters (m)	0.3
	yards (yd.)	meters	0.9
	miles (mi.)	kilometers (km)	1.6
Area	square inches (sq. in.)	square centimeters (sq cm)	6.5
	square feet (sq. ft.)	square meters (sq m)	0.09
	square yards (sq. yd.)	square meters	0.8
	square miles (sq. mi.)	square kilometers (sq km)	2.6
	acre (a.)	hectares (ha)	0.4
Volume	cubic inches (cu. in.)	cubic centimeters (cu cm)	16.4
	cubic feet (cu. ft.)	cubic meters (cu m)	0.028
	cubic yards (cu. yd.)	cubic meters	0.765
	cubic miles (cu. mi.)	cubic kilometers (cu km)	4.1
Weight	ounces (oz.)	grams (gm)	28.35
	pounds (lb.)	kilograms (kg)	0.45
	short tons	metric tons	0.9
Liquid Capacity	ounces (oz.)	milliliters (ml)	29.57
	pints (pt.)	liters (l)	0.47
	quarts (qt.)	liters	0.95
	gallons (gal.)	liters	3.8

Temperature To convert Fahrenheit (F) to Celsius (C), subtract 32, then multiply by 0.556.
To convert Celsius (C) to Fahrenheit (F), multiply by 1.8, then add 32.

Answer Key for Text Questions

The following pages list suggested answers for the questions that appear in the "As You Read," "Checking Up," and "Review Workshop" pages of the student text. These answers may serve as models when students' work is checked. Variant answers that the students can reasonably support should also be accepted.

Answers are grouped according to the units in which the questions appear in the student text. Student-text page numbers and the exercise titles under which the questions appear are also given for easy reference.

The key questions in the blue-tinted "As You Read" sections of the student text are repeated in the second to last question in the "Checking Up" section at the end of each chapter. Answers to these key questions are included with the "Checking Up" answers. Answers to the *Use this reading skill* activity are given when students are asked to respond to specific questions.

THE ATLAS TELLS A STORY
Checking Up (page 35)

1. One easy way to prove the earth is round is by watching a ship disappear on the horizon. A ship disappears slowly as it sails over the curved surface of the earth. If the earth had a sharp edge, a ship would disappear suddenly. However, the most dramatic proof of the earth's roundness can be seen in photographs taken from outer space (like the photograph on page 9). These photographs show conclusively that the earth is round.

2. In the Northern Hemisphere and in the Western Hemisphere.

3. 50° N. The equator is the starting point (0°) for parallels, or lines of latitude. The farther north one travels away from the equator, the higher the number of the parallel. So 50° N is farther from the equator than 30° N is.

4. One degree is equal to about 70 miles (112 km). So a location at 45° S is about 3,150 miles (5,040 km) south of the equator.

UNIT 1 AMERICA THE BEAUTIFUL
Checking Up (page 43)

1. Plains, plateaus, mountains, and hills.
2. Atlantic Ocean. Pacific Ocean.
3. Canada. Mexico.
4. Pictures of a huge cornfield with blue sky overhead; the Rocky Mountains with rolling plains in the foreground; a farmer harvesting wheat; a busy street intersection in a major city showing people, cars, and high-rise buildings; people of all races joined hand in hand; and huge ocean waves breaking. Other answers that the students can reasonably support should also be accepted.

Checking Up (page 47)

1. The freedom for Americans to choose any religion they wish to follow.

2. The freedom for Americans to write and speak their ideas and opinions.

3. The freedom to vote is a precious freedom that Americans enjoy, because not all people in the world have the right to choose their own community and national leaders.

4. The photographs illustrate how this country is full of variety. The photographs show different landscapes, life-styles, industries, and ethnic groups. Yet in the midst of all this diversity, we see Americans of all backgrounds working or celebrating together the history, traditions, and freedoms that are unique to this country. Other answers that the students can reasonably support should also be accepted.

5. All Americans enjoy the same freedoms in this country that no one can deny or take away, such as freedom of speech and freedom to vote. Americans all share the history and heritage of our country's past. At the same time, Americans have the same duty to work to protect our freedoms and maintain our country's best features for future generations of Americans. Other answers that the students can reasonably support should also be accepted.

TE 25

UNIT 1 REVIEW WORKSHOP
(pages 48–49)

What Have You Learned?

1. From New Mexico to Alaska.
2. The Atlantic, Pacific, and Arctic oceans.
3. Plains, plateaus, mountains, and hills. *Plains:* level or almost level lands; *plateaus:* high, flat lands, usually found between mountains; *mountains:* high, rocky lands, usually with steep sides and pointed or rounded tops; *hills:* rounded lands with sloping sides, smaller than mountains.
4. Hawaii and Washington.
5. Mississippi, Missouri, Delaware, Rio Grande, Platte, Snake, or Columbia. Other answers that the students can reasonably support should also be accepted.
6. Because of the great harvests from the rich farmlands on the Great Plains.

Use Your Reading Skills

While information on students' charts will vary, students should be encouraged to look at the following sections of their local newspaper: want ads, entertainment, and local news. Students should also look for human-interest stories that cover community events and celebrations.

Use Your Graphics-Reading Skills

1. Mountains, hills, and plains.
2. Grain crops and hay.
3. Because the land is cultivated. By farming.
4. While students' paragraphs will differ, students could point out that this area includes a river and its surrounding river valley. Cultivated fields dot the river valley. Rolling hills and mountains are also in this area.

UNIT 2 THE FIRST AMERICANS

Checking Up (page 55)

1. The American Indians are called the first Americans because they were the first group to migrate to the Americas.
2. About 1,400,000.
3. a. The influence of American Indians can be seen in thousands of place-names derived from Indian names, in the use of many medicines first developed by American Indians, and in the worldwide dependence on crops first developed and grown by Indian farmers.
    b. About half of all American Indians live on reservations. The rest live in a variety of settings—just like other Americans.
    c. Eskimos and Aleuts live in Alaska. Eskimos live in many parts of the state, but Aleuts live on the Aleutian Islands.
4. Many American Indians feel an attraction to the material wealth and progress of the modern United States and an attachment to the traditions of their past. These two feelings may account for the mix of the modern and the traditional on reservations. Other answers that the students can reasonably support should also be accepted.

Checking Up (page 59)

1. Asia. Across the Bering Strait into what is now Alaska.
2. They were probably following the animals they hunted.
3. Mountains.
4. Mountains, hills, plateaus, and plains. Plains have low elevation and low local relief. Plateaus have low local relief but are generally higher in elevation than plains. Mountains are high in both elevation and local relief. Hills are often worn-down mountains that have lower local relief than mountains.

Checking Up (page 64)

1. Eskimos and Aleuts.
2. The Mayas were an Indian tribe that lived in southern Mexico and parts of Middle America. They developed a rich culture. The Incas were an Indian tribe that lived in what is now Peru. They, too, developed a rich culture.
3. The tribes of the southeastern United States depended on the warm climate and rich soil of the region for their farming. They also hunted in the forests, gathered wild foods, and used wood for their homes.
4. a. As many of the large animals that the first Americans hunted disappeared, the first Americans began to depend more and more on plants and smaller animals for food. After learn-

ing more about plants, the first Americans began to farm. Soon they realized that farming provided a surer supply of food than hunting and gathering.

    b. Corn, white potatoes, squash, tomatoes, peppers, sweet potatoes, and beans.

    c. Climate and resources dictated the way Indians obtained their food—by farming or by hunting and gathering. Climate and resources dictated the type of homes Indians built and the clothes they wore. In fact, the climate and resources of an area still affect the way any group of people lives.

Checking Up (page 68)

1. Once the Navajo had learned to farm, they no longer had to depend completely on hunting and gathering for their food.

2. The Spanish called these Indians the Pueblo because the Indians lived in villages. *Pueblo* is the Spanish word for "village."

3. The Pueblo grew more food than they needed. They traded this surplus food, along with baskets, pottery, and jewelry, to other Indian tribes.

4. a. In what is now the states of Arizona, New Mexico, Utah, Colorado, and Texas.

    b. The Pueblo irrigated their farms because the area in which they lived has a dry climate that makes farming difficult.

    c. The Navajo changed from a strictly hunting and gathering culture to include farming in their food production. They also learned weaving from the Pueblo and herding from the Spanish colonists.

5. The Navajo probably saw that the Pueblo had made a remarkable adaptation to the conditions of the Southwest. The Navajo incorporated some of the Pueblo ways to adapt to the Southwest. Other answers that the students can reasonably support should also be accepted.

Checking Up (page 72)

1. The Mandan lived near the Missouri River in what is now North Dakota and South Dakota. The Crow lived near the headwaters of the Yellowstone River. The Shoshone lived in the Great Basin.

2. The Crow used hides for tepees and clothing, bones for tools, tongues for hairbrushes, hair for stuffing pillows, tails for flyswatters, and hooves for making glue. Buffalo meat was the staple of the Crow diet.

3. a. Farming, hunting, and gathering.

    b. The horse made Plains Indians more mobile and, consequently, more able to follow the enormous herds of buffalo. As a result, the homes of the nomadic tribes had to be portable, as the tepee was. Other answers that the students can reasonably support should also be accepted.

    c. Agricultural tribes like the Mandan built earth lodges. Nomadic tribes like the Crow built tepees.

4. The buffalo were the main resource readily available to the Crow. The buffalo weren't simply the main food resource; they were the main clothing and shelter resource on the plains at that time.

Checking Up (page 76)

1. The peace chiefs were the political leaders of the Iroquois; the war chiefs had authority only during war.

2. The forests provided Eastern Woodland tribes with wood and bark for their homes and their canoes. Plants in the forests were used for food and clothing. The animals in the forests provided both food and clothing.

3. Wigwams were built by constructing a framework of thin poles that were covered first by branches, then by mats of woven cattails, and finally by sheets of tree bark.

4. a. Corn.

    b. The Iroquois League was an organization of five (later six) tribes that settled arguments among families, clans, and tribes.

    c. Iroquois women chose (and sometimes dismissed) the chiefs of the clans to which they belonged. Since the clan chiefs led each tribe, women had significant political power in the tribal council.

5. The Iroquois League helped end feuding among the various groups of people within the league. As with any large organization, there was probably exchange of information and goods that

benefited all concerned. Other answers that the students can reasonably support should also be accepted.

As You Read (page 77)
Use this reading skill.

Abundant means "in great supply." Students should be able to ascertain the meaning of *abundant* by reading that most of the needs of Northwest Coast Indians were supplied by forest products.

Checking Up (page 79)

1. Fish, particularly salmon.
2. The host of the potlatch gave away presents to everyone attending. Sometimes hosts would give away everything they owned.
3. Totem poles were a means that Northwest Coast Indians had for telling people the story of their ancestors.
4. a. Fish, shellfish, and forest and mountain animals.

    b. Homes were constructed of wood and contained many "apartments" so many families could live in one house. In the center of the house on the ground floor was a large, open space that families used for cooking. The apartments were one level above this center area.

    c. The construction of totem poles and the potlatch ceremony were two aspects that set Northwest Coast Indians apart from the rest of the Indians in what is now the United States.
5. The use of wood products for homes and even clothing was an adaptation influenced by the abundance of wood in this area. The abundance of wood is a result of the rainy climate. Other answers that the students can reasonably support should also be accepted.

UNIT 2 REVIEW WORKSHOP (pages 80–81)

What Have You Learned?

1. The first people to live in the Americas were hunters from Asia. Archaeologists believe these people migrated here because the first Americans were following the animals they hunted.
2. A reservation is land that belongs to a tribe or tribes. West of the Mississippi River.
3. Incan and Mayan cultures. Both groups were expert farmers and builders. The Mayas were skilled in astronomy and mathematics. The Incas were experts in jewelry crafting and in road building.
4. The Pueblo built large, apartmentlike homes made of stone or adobe. The homes of the Pueblo were taller than those of the Mandan.
5. Horses made Plains Indians more mobile and made buffalo hunting possible over a much wider area.
6. Corn, beans, squash, and game. Fish and shellfish as well as game and nuts and berries.
7. The Crow and Indians of the Northwest Coast. These Indians did not farm because food resources in their areas were so abundant that farming was not necessary to ensure an adequate food supply.

Use Your Reading Skills

The study of human beings. The study of the earth.

Use Your Map Skills

1. Mohawk. Seneca.
2. The Erie, the Huron, the Mahican, and the Delaware. The Mahican and the Delaware. The Erie and the Huron.
3. The Mohawk River, Lake Oneida, Lake Onondaga, Lake Cayuga, and Lake Seneca.

Use Your Thinking Skills

1. The Iroquois.
2. The Crow.

UNIT 3 EXPLORING THE NEW WORLD

As You Read (page 84)
Use this reading skill.

The topic sentence is "About 1,500 years ago, some people in China believed that a land lay to the east, beyond the great sea." The rest of the paragraph explains what this land may have been.

TE 28

Checking Up (page 87)

1. An Icelander named Eric the Red and some of his family and friends.

2. An archaeologist named Helge Ingstad found in Newfoundland the foundations of homes like those built by the Norse in Greenland. Ingstad also found implements made in Norway about the year 1000.

3. a. There is a written Chinese report about Fu-sang, the land that lay to the east of China. To some archaeologists, this report seems to describe North America rather than Japan. The presence of a strong ocean current moving from the Chinese coast to the North American coast makes some archaeologists think that such a trip was possible.

   b. The Icelanders or Norse.

   c. Ingstad discovered the remains of a Norse settlement in Newfoundland.

4. The Norse sagas provide a reasonably accurate description of the coast of southeastern Canada. The sagas also give information about the colony established by Leif Ericson. Since the sagas contain accurate information about the Norse colony in Greenland, it seems likely to historians that some of the information about Vinland was also true.

Checking Up (page 91)

1. Marco Polo was an Italian merchant whose description of the goods available in China stimulated European interest in travel to Asia.

2. Portugal.

3. a. In southeastern Asia.

   b. The Europeans wanted to obtain spices and silk—but especially spices.

   c. At that time, the Turks captured Constantinople, which was the principal shipping point through which Asian goods went to Europe. The Turks closed the port to Europeans, who then had to find a new route to Asia.

4. Most people in Columbus's time thought that sailing around Africa was the easiest way to travel to Asia. The Atlantic Ocean was an unknown, uncharted vastness. Columbus thought (incorrectly!) that sailing across the Atlantic would be a much easier, faster way to get to Asia.

Checking Up (page 94)

1. He planned to start a trading colony.

2. a. Columbus thought that Asia was only 2,400 miles (3,840 km) from the Canary Islands. Actually, Asia is about 11,000 miles (16,960 km) from the Canary Islands.

   b. Queen Isabella and King Ferdinand of Spain.

   c. Columbus ordered food for the journey, stored it safely on the ships, and chose a crew.

3. Although Columbus may have been intimidated by the real distance between Europe and Asia, he still did not know that two continents lie between Europe and Asia. So he may have persisted in his plan. Other answers that the students can reasonably support should also be accepted.

Checking Up (page 98)

1. Columbus believed that he had landed in the Indies, so he called the people he met there *Indians*.

2. The two most critical problems were the settlers' unwillingness to build homes and plant crops and the diseases that killed hundreds of settlers.

3. Cuba, Hispaniola, and parts of South America. Other answers that the students can reasonably support should also be accepted.

4. a. On San Salvador, a small island in the Bahamas.

   b. Four.

   c. People thought Columbus's discoveries were worthless because he had not reached the spice-rich Indies nor had he found any great amounts of gold or silver.

5. Columbus's understanding of geography made it seem that what he had discovered had to be Asia. He simply could not accept that there were two enormous continents of which the rest of the world had been ignorant until 1492. Other answers that the students can reasonably support should also be accepted.

Checking Up (page 107)

1. The lands that are now the states of New Mexico and Arizona.

TE 29

2. Coronado claimed the southwest part of what is now the United States, and de Soto claimed the southeast part.

3. a. Like Columbus, Magellan thought the best way of reaching Asia was to cross the Atlantic Ocean and then the Pacific Ocean.

b. Cortes, an army of about 600 Spanish soldiers, and several thousand Indians who wanted to be free from Aztec rule.

c. Coronado and de Soto claimed land in North America for Spain.

4. Perhaps the overriding concern of the Spanish was to enrich their own country by taking valuable commodities out of their New World empire. Yet the Spanish were also eager to spread the Christian religion. And many of the individuals who came to the New World were eager for adventure and glory. Other answers that the students can reasonably support should also be accepted.

Checking Up (page 111)

1. John Cabot.
2. Quebec, Canada.
3. a. Many Europeans thought that Columbus's idea of sailing across the Atlantic to reach the Indies was the right way of reaching Asia easily. However, many thought that the easiest way across the Atlantic to Asia would be through a "Northwest Passage." So the Northwest Passage was yet another instance of the belief that an easy all-water route to Asia could be found.

b. The two French explorers were Jacques Cartier and Samuel de Champlain.

c. The area around the Hudson River in what is now New York State. The area around Hudson Bay in what is now Canada.

4. Perhaps the greatest disappointment for many explorers was that they were unable to find an easy all-water route to the Indies. The hardships of sailing through unknown waters to unknown lands were great—many explorers, like Cabot, simply disappeared. Other answers that the students can reasonably support should also be accepted. Discuss with students the problems of exposure, starvation, and disease that many early explorers faced.

UNIT 3 REVIEW WORKSHOP (pages 112–113)

What Have You Learned?

1. An archaeologist named Helge Ingstad discovered the remains of a Norse settlement in Newfoundland.
2. The Turks, with their capture of the port of Constantinople in the late 1400s, cut off the principal route between Asia and Europe. In addition, travel by sea was far easier than any other means of transportation.
3. Four.
4. Magellan.
5. Spain.
6. England, France, and the Netherlands.

Use Your Reading Skills

1. Cortes landed in Mexico.
2. England.
3. Cartier.
4. Hudson.

Use Your Speaking Skills

1. Magellan sailed around the world. Were the world any other shape, Magellan could not have sailed fully around it.

2–3. Magellan's travels proved there were thousands of miles between the Americas, where Columbus landed, and Asia.

Use Your Map Skills

1. The area that is now Florida in the United States.
2. South America.
3. Middle America, particularly the area that is now Panama.

UNIT 4 COLONIES IN NORTH AMERICA

Checking Up (page 119)

1. Don Juan de Oñate.
2. a. The Spanish wanted to find new gold and silver mines. They also wanted to bring Spanish rule to the land of the Pueblo and to convert the Indians to the Christian religion.

b. They demanded that the Pueblo accept Spanish rule.

c. Spain established settlements in the present-day states of New Mexico, Texas, California, and Florida.

3. Most of the needs of the people were provided for on both missions and haciendas. Some of the people who lived on missions and haciendas were not free. The Spanish made many of the Indians who lived and worked on haciendas servants or slaves. The Indians living on missions were not free to leave. Life on haciendas did not center around church activities, as it did on missions. Other answers that the students can reasonably support should also be accepted.

Checking Up (page 123)

1. A group of Puritans who later became known as the Pilgrims.

2. A Powhatan princess. Pocahontas urged the leaders of her tribe to help the colonists at Jamestown.

3. a. Jamestown, Virginia.

b. Finding a good site for a colony, finding ways for settlers to make a living, keeping peace with nearby Indian tribes, making the colony a financial success, or attracting more settlers to the colony. Other answers that the students can reasonably support should also be accepted.

c. They wanted to live in a place where they could have religious freedom. While in England, the Puritans had been forced to belong to the Church of England, which they did not want to do.

4. While both groups of colonists made friendship agreements with nearby Indian tribes, only the Plymouth colonists kept their agreements. In addition, the Plymouth colonists invited the Wampanoag tribe to a feast to give thanks for the Indians' help and for a good harvest. On the other hand, the Jamestown colonists broke their agreements with the Powhatan tribe. The Powhatan became enemies when the colonists began to steal the Indians' food. For a while peace was restored, but then the colonists again failed to keep the peace. Other answers that the students can reasonably support should also be accepted.

Checking Up (page 127)

1. A mapmaker.

2. By using small drawings of hills and mountains of different sizes. By using shades of black and different colors.

Checking Up (page 131)

1. Louis Joliet, Father Jacques Marquette, and Robert de La Salle.

2. a. The fur trade.

b. Lands around the St. Lawrence River, the Great Lakes, and the entire Mississippi River valley.

c. In 1664 the English captured the Dutch colony of New Netherland. There was no resistance from Dutch colonists.

3. The French generally treated Indians well, and in turn, Indians kept peace with the French. For example, the French made fur-trading agreements with Indians that benefited both sides. The French traded goods wanted by the Indians for valuable furs. In addition, the French generally did not clear the Indians' land for settlements but instead left the land intact, which pleased the Indians. Moreover, the French sent missionaries to live and work with the Indians. The missionaries usually treated the Indians well, and as a result, many friendships were made. Other answers that the students can reasonably support should also be accepted.

Checking Up (page 136)

1. A Puritan minister who, dissatisfied with rule in the Massachusetts Bay Colony, left the colony and founded the colony of Rhode Island.

2. The rocky soil and short summers in New England made it difficult for most farmers to grow any more crops than what would feed their families.

3. a. Georgia, South Carolina, North Carolina, Virginia, Maryland, Delaware, Pennsylvania, New Jersey, New York, Connecticut, Rhode Island, Massachusetts, and New Hampshire.

b. Men and women who agreed to come to the colonies to work for a person for five or more years in exchange for their travel expenses, housing, and jobs.

c. Because more and more people were needed to work on the growing number of large plantations in the Southern colonies.

4. *Similarities:* Most people earned a living by farming. Slaves worked in all the colonies. Many colonial crops or products were shipped to England. *Differences:* While most farmers in the New England and Middle colonies grew just enough to feed their families, southern farmers usually grew great amounts of one crop to sell. Many products were grown or produced in certain colonies depending on those colonies' locations, such as forest products from New England and cotton and rice from the South. Other answers that the students can reasonably support should also be accepted.

Checking Up (page 140)

1. The House of Burgesses in Virginia.
2. A young person who lived and worked with a master of a craft to learn a trade. After the apprenticeship was over, the young person could open a shop.
3. a. Each colony had some form of representative government, a legislature that passed laws, and voting restrictions. Other answers that the students can reasonably support should also be accepted.

b. Farming, making bread, shearing sheep, weaving cloth from homespun wool, or building homes. Other answers that the students can reasonably support should also be accepted.

c. Because colonial roads were so poor that many people and colonial crops and goods traveled by boat.

4. *More difficult:* Less time was spent on entertainment and leisure activities because so many families, especially on farms, spent almost all their time and energy producing things they needed to live. More time was needed to travel because of poor roads and slower means of transportation. People's lives were often governed by the amount of daylight each day because there was no electricity, only whale oil lamps or costly candles. There was no running water or indoor bathrooms. Most children had the chance to attend school only a few years or not at all. *Easier:* People had more control over their lives because they made almost everything they needed. Life was often simpler because fewer decisions had to be made. Life is more complicated today because of technological advances in communication and transportation. People today have to make more decisions about what kind of job to train for and where they want to live. Other answers that the students can reasonably support should also be accepted.

Checking Up (page 143)

1. Don Diego de Vargas.
2. a. The Pequot War and King Philip's War.

b. Tribes of the Southeast formed alliances with various European nations fighting in the area for its control. Eventually thousands of Indians who had joined these alliances died in the Europeans' border struggles.

c. The last of the Spanish colonists left New Mexico and fled south. However, the Spanish recaptured New Mexico twelve years later.

3. As the population in the European colonies increased, more and more Europeans settled new lands farther inland. As a result, many Indians were pushed away from their homelands or died trying to stop the spread of European settlements. Also, thousands of Indians died of diseases brought by Europeans. Still other Indians died fighting as allies of various European nations in European border struggles in North America. Other answers that the students can reasonably support should also be accepted.

UNIT 4 REVIEW WORKSHOP (pages 144–145)

What Have You Learned?

1. Don Juan de Oñate.
2. Because Spanish explorers in North America, unlike those in Middle and South America, did not find rich treasures such as gold and silver mines.
3. Jamestown, Virginia.
4. Fur trading and exploring.
5. New York.
6. By farming.
7. The Pequot War and King Philip's War.

Use Your Reading Skills

New England Colonies: Plymouth, Anne Hutchinson, Mayflower Compact, shipbuilding, Boston.

Middle Colonies: William Penn, New York, New Amsterdam, Quakers, New Jersey.

Southern Colonies: Jamestown, plantations, House of Burgesses, Powhatan.

Use Your Map Skills

1. In the present-day Southwest and in what is now Florida.
2. Along the Atlantic seaboard.
3. Florida.
4. Mississippi River, St. Lawrence River, and all the Great Lakes.
5. France.

Use Your Math Skills

1. Seventy years.
2. About 5,000 more.
3. Between 1680 and 1690.
4. About 205,000 more.

UNIT 5 CREATING A NEW NATION

Checking Up (page 151)

1. Because the British claimed these same lands and had set up companies to develop fur trading and farming in the Ohio River valley.

2. France gave Great Britain New France and the land between the Appalachians and the Mississippi River. France gave Spain the port of New Orleans and all the French lands west of the Mississippi River.

3. The Huron and Algonquin. The Iroquois.

4. a. In 1749 the French posted markers in the Ohio River valley, and in 1753 the French built forts in the same area to protect their claim to the valley.

   b. Because many British settlers wanted to move to lands west of the Appalachians to gain more farmland, a greater share of the fur trade, and safety for their frontier settlements.

   c. It proved that the British had won the right to control eastern North America.

5. This was a time of national expansion, when powerful countries such as Great Britain, France, and Spain fought to control as much land in the world as possible. Because Britain already controlled a part of eastern North America along the Atlantic seaboard, it seemed natural to many people in Britain to control the entire eastern half of North America. Besides, this was land that the British claimed was theirs. And at the same time, closer to home, many British colonists who lived east of the Appalachians wanted to move farther west across the mountains. They wanted more farmland and a greater share of the profitable fur trade controlled by the French. These colonists probably pressured the leaders in Britain to expand British control to the Mississippi River. Other answers that the students can reasonably support should also be accepted.

Checking Up (page 155)

1. Other European countries, Africa, or the West Indies.

2. *New England colonies:* ships, fish, bars of iron, lumber, whale by-products, or naval stores; *Middle colonies:* grain, meat, furs, lumber, bars of iron, or ships; *Southern colonies:* tobacco, rice, indigo, furs and deerskins, naval stores, fish, or bars of iron. Students should be encouraged to use both the text and the map on page 153 to answer this question.

3. a. They were the five largest colonial cities, the centers of colonial trade, and seaports with harbors on bays or rivers leading to the ocean.

   b. Raw materials such as lumber, tobacco, or furs.

   c. Manufactured goods such as nails, farm tools, glass, or cloth.

4. Because the seaports' locations on waterways made them natural stops for ships, which transported most colonial trade. Ships could conveniently dock at the seaports' harbors to load or unload trading goods. Other answers that the students can reasonably support should also be accepted.

As You Read (page 156)

Use this reading skill.

By the mid-1700s, an uneasy peace had developed between many colonists and the British concerning British rule of the thirteen colonies. Many Patriots saw the killing of four colonists in 1770 as one more instance of British antagonism. However, people in Britain, wanting no further trouble in the colonies, tried to keep this incident from being blown out of proportion. Other answers that the students can reasonably support should also be accepted.

Checking Up (page 160)

1. British goods such as stamps or tea.

2. In 1768 more British troops were sent to Boston. In March 1770 the Boston Massacre occured. In 1773 the Boston Tea Party happened. Afterward, the king closed the port of Boston. Other answers that the students can reasonably support should also be accepted.

3. a. Because the king declared all lands west of the Appalachians to be Indian land.

   b. Because for the first time in colonial history, Parliament passed a tax to raise money that was not approved by the colonial assemblies before it went into effect. And for the first time, many colonists became very angry about British rule. Some took violent action; others showed their anger by boycotting British goods. Still others organized the first meeting of all the colonies in colonial history to discuss the Stamp Act. Other answers that the students can reasonably support should also be accepted.

   c. Because representatives from almost every colony met to discuss recent actions taken by the king against the colonists and to decide a course of action.

4. Because the colonists were not allowed any representation in Parliament, many colonists believed that they should not have to pay taxes that were passed by Parliament. The colonists' only say in government was through their elected representatives who made up the colonial assemblies. In the past Parliament had submitted tax laws to the colonial assemblies before the taxes became law. However, when Parliament passed taxes such as the Stamp Act without first approval by the colonial assemblies, the colonists were completely left out of the lawmaking process. Many colonists then refused to pay the taxes that they had not approved. Other answers that the students can reasonably support should also be accepted.

Checking Up (page 165)

1. People who had drilled and promised "to fight on a minute's notice" in the event of a war between the thirteen colonies and Britain. At the first battle of the Revolutionary War at Lexington, Massachusetts, and at later battles of the war.

2. Thomas Jefferson. The delegates of the Second Continental Congress. Philadelphia, Pennsylvania.

3. a. The delegates of the Second Continental Congress accepted the Declaration of Independence, which signaled the birth of a new country—the United States of America.

   b. The battles of Saratoga and Yorktown.

   c. France, Spain, and the Netherlands.

4. Because the allies of the new United States gave this country great moral, military, and financial support when it was struggling to exist as an independent nation and defeat one of the most powerful nations in the world. Moral support from France, Spain, and the Netherlands encouraged the United States to win the war. French military support through its army, navy, and the great General Lafayette helped the United States defeat Great Britain. Finally, financial support in the form of money, clothing, and firearms provided needed supplies and money to win the war and keep the new United States government running. Other answers that the students can reasonably support should also be accepted.

Checking Up (page 169)

1. The problems of who would govern these lands, of British and Spanish forts still on United States soil, and/or of Indians and settlers living in these same lands, often at war with each other.

2. Congress makes laws, approves appointments made by the President, and declares war. The President suggests laws, approves or disapproves laws passed by Congress, and sees that the laws are carried out.

3. a. To write a constitution, or plan of government, for the United States.

b. The legislative, executive, and judicial branches.

c. The first ten amendments to the Constitution, which guarantee that certain freedoms and rights of United States citizens can never be taken away.

4. While students' answers will differ, students should be encouraged to use the "Powers" section of the chart on page 168 to answer the first part of the question and the "Limits" section of the chart to answer the second part. For example, the making of a law involves all three branches. Congress makes the law but is limited in that the President can refuse to approve the law or the Supreme Court can do away with the law if it does not follow the Constitution. In this example it is important that all three branches have some say so that a law that would be unfair to the people would not become a law. In general, it is important that the branches work together so that no one branch will ever be stronger or more powerful than the other two. Other answers that the students can reasonably support should also be accepted.

Checking Up (page 177)

1. Served as the first chief justice of the Supreme Court and negotiated a treaty with Britain to remove its troops from United States soil.

2. To help the U.S. ally France defeat Britain, to force Britain to give up its forts and remove its troops from United States land, or to force British troops to stop inciting and arming Indians in the Ohio River valley. Other answers that the students can reasonably support should also be accepted.

3. a. To take office as the first President of the United States.

b. Because treasury workers collected taxes on goods shipped to and from the United States and these taxes kept the government running and paid its bills.

c. The signing of a treaty by Indians in the Ohio River valley in which they gave up all their land east of the Mississippi River and between the Great Lakes and the Ohio River and the signing of a treaty by the British in which they agreed to remove their troops from the United States.

4. With the removal of Indians from the Ohio River valley, Americans could safely settle the rich farmland in the Ohio River valley. In time, these pioneer settlements became the foundation for future states in that area of the country. Other answers that the students can reasonably support should also be accepted.

UNIT 5 REVIEW WORKSHOP (pages 178–179)

What Have You Learned?

1. *Britain:* all lands east of the Mississippi River except the port of New Orleans; *Spain:* the port of New Orleans and all the lands west of the Mississippi River; *France:* no lands in North America.

2. Raw materials and manufactured goods. *Raw materials:* lumber, tobacco, furs, cotton; *manufactured goods:* ships, flour. Other answers that the students can reasonably support should also be accepted.

3. They believed that only the colonial assemblies should have the right to tax the colonies, but in this instance, Parliament had passed the Stamp Act without the approval of the colonial assemblies.

4. Because the delegates to the Second Continental Congress had asked Jefferson to write a declaration listing the colonists' complaints against the king and the rights of the colonists to live in a new country free of British rule.

5. The legislative, executive, and judicial branches. *Legislative branch:* makes the laws, approves appointments made by the President, or declares war; *executive branch:* suggests laws, approves or disapproves laws passed by Congress, or sees that the laws are carried out; *judicial branch:* decides if a law disagrees with the U.S. Constitution, decides cases between states, or judges whether people's rights have been taken away. Other answers that the students can reasonably support should also be accepted.

6. An amendment either adds to or takes out a part of the Constitution. The Bill of Rights.

7. Delivered a message from the governor of Virginia to the French to leave the Ohio River valley, led the colonial militia during the French and Indian War, served as commander in chief of the Continental Army during the Revolutionary War, served as president of the Constitutional Convention, and served two four-year terms as the first President of the United States. Other answers that the students can reasonably support should also be accepted.

Use Your Reading Skills

1. Opinion. There was never any law or decree passed by the British Parliament or ruler giving the colonists the sole power to tax themselves.

2. Fact. This fact is found in the chapter entitled: "Breaking Ties with Britain."

3. Opinion. Many colonists felt the tax was unfair because it had not been approved by the colonial assemblies. However, Parliament had the right to tax the thirteen colonies whether the colonists liked it or not.

4. Opinion. This is a judgment of someone by someone else. Perhaps many British people felt the colonists were lawbreakers, but many colonists felt they had a right to disobey laws they considered unjust.

5. Fact. The word *innocent* may seem to make this statement an opinion. However, the text says the young Bostonians were only teasing and throwing sticks and snowballs at the British troops. The colonists were not armed; they could not have defended themselves against the British shots.

6. Fact. Although many colonists would have disagreed, Parliament, as stated in the text, was the British lawmaking body and had the authority to pass laws such as taxes over any territory ruled by Britain, including the thirteen American colonies.

7. Fact. According to the text, closing the port imposed great hardships on Bostonians and others who depended on goods being moved through Boston Harbor.

Students may give other reasons for their answers, which should be accepted if the students can reasonably support them.

Use Your Map Skills

1. Delaware Bay and the Atlantic Ocean.
2. Delaware River.
3. A political border.
4. The Appalachian Mountains.
5. All thirteen colonies except Pennsylvania had some area bordering the Atlantic Ocean.

Use Your Thinking Skills

1. Furniture, candlesticks, and other wooden goods for homes.
2. Saws, hammers, awls, files, chisels, and a sharpening stone. Other answers that the students can reasonably support should also be accepted.
3. Saws and hammers.
4. Because many of the items now are made by machines and this decreases the time needed to make the items. Other answers that the students can reasonably support should also be accepted.

UNIT 6 LOOKING WESTWARD

As You Read (page 182)
Use this reading skill.

All the listed "causes"—the Erie Canal, the National Road, and the *Clermont*—had much the same effect: they improved transportation to the Northwest Territory. The Erie Canal made travel to the Great Lakes much easier and thus opened up the northern part of the Northwest Territory to many thousands of people. The National Road connected the more settled areas of the former colonies to the Ohio River and thereby made travel easier to the southern part of the Northwest Territory. Thousands of pioneers used the National Road to travel to Ohio, Indiana, and Illinois. The development of the steamboat, of which the *Clermont* was the first successful model, also made travel to the west easier and ultimately more affordable, so many families could join in the westward migration.

Checking Up (page 185)

1. The Northwest Territory, Kentucky, and the Southwest Territory.

2. The Northwest Territory is now the states of Ohio, Indiana, Illinois, Wisconsin, and Michigan. The Southwest Territory is now the state of Tennessee and parts of Georgia, Alabama, and Mississippi.

3. a. An area was first explored by a few hunters and trappers. Later, pioneer families moved into the area and developed it for farming. As the number of families grew, towns also developed to provide goods and services for the farm families.

b. There were many important developments in the early 1800s that helped the settlement of the United States. The building of a system of canals and roads made it easier for thousands of settlers to reach newly opened territory. The application of steam power to ships brought about the invention of the steamboat. These new modes of transportation not only made travel easier and faster but also made the shipping of goods easier and faster. As a result, settlers in the new territories could buy and sell goods more easily than before. This aid to commerce was also an aid to settlement.

c. Transportation by water was the easiest and cheapest form of transportation in the early 1800s. In particular, it was easier to ship bulky goods by water than by land.

4. With the opening of the Erie Canal, New York City became a port on the Great Lakes as well as being a port on the Atlantic Ocean. Agricultural goods from Great Lakes states could be shipped to New York City, while manufactured goods from New York City could be shipped to Great Lakes states. The markets for New York City's goods had increased dramatically. The prosperity the Erie Canal brought helped the city grow.

Checking Up (page 190)

1. The Louisiana Purchase and the purchase of Florida.

2. Lewis and Clark and Columbus wanted to find an all-water route to Asia. Both groups knew part, but not all, of their routes. Both groups were uncertain where their travels would take them.

3. Crossing the Rocky Mountains.

4. a. The Louisiana Purchase doubled the size of our country. With this purchase, the United States controlled the Mississippi River, an important natural highway, and the Mississippi's most important port, New Orleans. In addition, many people thought there might be an all-water route to Asia that passed through the Louisiana Purchase.

b. Lewis and Clark followed the Missouri River to what is now Great Falls, Montana. They then followed other rivers through the Rockies until they reached the Columbia River. They canoed down the Columbia to the Pacific Ocean.

c. Florida and the lands owned by Indians in the southeastern United States.

5. Lewis and Clark and Pike were able to obtain accurate information about the lands through which they traveled. This information helped settlers decide where and how to travel through and in these lands. Perhaps more important, these explorers excited the imaginations of settlers; their reports of the wonders they had seen made people want to settle in the "new" lands.

Checking Up (page 194)

1. A physical map uses color and gray shading to show the elevations and landforms of an area.

2. A contour map also shows the elevations and landforms of an area. However, a contour map uses lines and numbers instead of color and gray shading to show elevation and local relief.

3. The closer together different contour lines are, the steeper a particular hill or mountain is.

4. Plains and plateaus show up on a contour map as areas in which there are a few widely separated contour lines. The numbers on the contour lines of a plains area will be lower than those of a plateau area because the numbers reflect elevation and plains are lower in elevation than plateaus. Hills and mountains show up on a contour map as areas in which there are many contour lines that are close together. Seeing these lines close together informs you that there is

great local relief. The numbers on the contour lines of a mountainous area will be higher than the numbers on the contour lines of a hilly area; in addition, the contour lines on a map of a mountainous area will be closer together than the contour lines on a map of a hilly area.

As You Read (page 195)
Use this reading skill.

Both Texas and Oregon were areas owned by countries other than the United States in the early 1800s. However, settlers from the United States poured into both areas. Eventually, the presence of so many Americans made the acquisition of these territories important to the United States government.

Checking Up (page 198)

1. Stephen Austin led the first group of U.S. settlers into Texas.

2. After Texas won its independence from Mexico, it was annexed to the United States. California became part of the United States as part of the settlement with Mexico after the Mexican War.

3. After gold was discovered in California in 1848, thousands of people came to California to look for gold.

4. a. Most settlers in Texas were used to the laws and customs of the United States.

  b. Texas, Oregon, and Washington, and the area that now includes the states of New Mexico, Arizona, California, Nevada, and parts of Utah and Colorado.

  c. The Santa Fe and Old Spanish trails were important to settlers of the Southwest. The Oregon, California, and Mormon trails were important to settlers of other parts of the West.

5. The traders and trappers were among the first to mark trails that were later used by pioneer families. In addition, traders and trappers often led the wagon trains on the trails west.

Checking Up (page 203)

1. The way the pioneers depended on game animals and corn for food paralleled the way the Indians also depended on these foodstuffs.

2. Log cabins were generally one-room homes constructed of rough logs held together with mud. Floors were made of wooden planks or packed dirt. There were few windows in most cabins; most often, these windows were covered not by glass but by animal skins or greased paper. Fireplaces provided heat for homes as well as for cooking.

3. a. The pioneers were people from the United States and from many other countries.

  b. Generally, pioneers went west with the hope that they could find a better life. This "better life" might consist of better soil for farming, a more congenial climate, riches in the form of gold, or simply solitude. Other answers that the students can reasonably support should also be accepted.

  c. Pioneer life was difficult and demanding. All of the pioneers' needs had to be met by the pioneers themselves. Students should be able to discuss the specifics of pioneer travel, homes, and food production after reading this chapter.

4. Since pioneer life was difficult and pioneers were venturing into the unknown, there was a need for some sort of reassurance provided by the familiar. If an entire group of people could travel and settle together, they could provide one another with some small measure of comfort and reassurance.

Checking Up (page 207)

1. Great Britain.

2. The growth of the textile industry increased demand for cotton grown in the South.

3. The McCormick reaper.

4. a. The textile industry.

  b. The industrial revolution had an enormous impact on farming in the United States. There were the changes in the methods of farming itself; the reaper, for example, greatly increased how much grain could be harvested. There were changes in the way farm crops were processed; the cotton gin, for example, greatly increased the amount of cotton that could be cleaned. In addition, there were changes brought about in factories that had an impact on farming; for example, the increased ability to produce cotton thread and cloth created an enormous demand for cotton. Finally, there were changes created by changes; the success of the reaper decreased the need for agricultural workers, many of whom went to work in factories.

c. Many of the most important innovations of the industrial revolution—the cotton gin, interchangeable parts, the reaper, and the telegraph—were the ideas of U.S. inventors.

5. Some of the inventions, such as the railroad and the telegraph, brought the country closer together by making travel and communication faster. Yet the innovations of the industrial revolution also made the economies of the different regions dependent on one another. A national economy began to emerge during this period.

Checking Up (page 211)

1. They believed it was wrong for one person to own another.

2. It was a meeting for people who wanted to obtain the right to vote for women.

3. a. Slaves were the basis of farm labor in the South. Slaves were the people who planted, harvested, and cleaned cotton.

b. They wanted to abolish slavery.

c. Woman suffrage means women's right to vote.

4. Former slaves were personally aware of the evils of slavery. Other answers that the students can reasonably support should also be accepted.

UNIT 6 REVIEW WORKSHOP (pages 212–213)

What Have You Learned?

1. Each helped improve transportation to the West.

2. Francis Scott Key. 1813.

3. Lewis and Clark were looking for an all-water route to Asia as well as exploring the newly purchased Louisiana Territory.

4. Pike explored what is now Missouri, Arkansas, Oklahoma, Colorado, and New Mexico.

5. The United States purchased a large amount of land from Mexico at the end of the Mexican War. This purchase included what is now New Mexico and Arizona.

6. Most pioneers lived in one-room log cabins. These simple homes were made of rough logs patched with mud. Floors were wooden planks or packed dirt. The few windows were often covered by animal skins or greased paper. The fireplace was the most important spot in the cabin because it served as both furnace and kitchen.

7. They were built with large wheels to move well on muddy roads. The high ends of the wagons prevented goods from falling out. The boat shape of the wagons helped keep loads stable.

8. The cotton gin and interchangeable parts.

9. They were people who favored abolishing slavery.

10. They believed women should have more rights, including the right to vote.

Use Your Reading Skills

With your feet. On foot. A *centipede* is an insect that appears to have 100 feet. A *pedestal* is a support or foundation for something, as feet are supports for people. A *pedometer* is a device that measures distances traveled on foot. A pedigree is a family tree, or list of ancestors. *Pedigree* originally meant "foot of a crane" (a crane is a type of bird). A family tree is sometimes shaped like a bird's foot.

Use Your Time Skills

1. Kentucky. Ohio.

2. These states had small, widely scattered populations.

3. 1820–1830.

4. 1820–1830.

Use Your Thinking Skills

1. False. The Natchez Trace was a north-south thoroughfare. Other answers that the students can reasonably support should also be accepted.

2. False. The Natchez Trace was not in one of the original colonies, yet it was in operation by 1815.

3. False. There were no canals that far west by 1815.

4. False. Students should be able to point out canals that connected rivers to rivers.

5. False. The states that had been colonies had about as many roads and canals as the states that had made up the Northwest Territory.

TE 39

UNIT 7 WAR AND A NEW BEGINNING

Checking Up (page 218)

1. *Transportation:* Because each section's need for transportation was different. In the North, where there were many factories, business owners wanted more transportation built to ship their products to other parts of the country. However, in the South, where there were many waterways and good seaports to ship products, many southerners saw no need to build new roads and railroads. *Tariffs:* Because each section had a different amount of manufacturing, which was affected by tariffs. The North's many factory owners wanted tariffs to protect their goods from foreign competition. However, southerners, who had few factories, were against tariffs because they wanted to buy manufactured goods from Europe as well as from the North.

2. a. The North, South, and West. In location, development, economic life, population, political issues such as transportation, taxes, or slavery. Other answers that the students can reasonably support should also be accepted.

   b. *Disagreements over transportation:* The North wanted the government to spend more money to improve transportation. The North's many factory owners said new roads and railroads would make it easier to ship their manufactured goods to other parts of the country. The South did not need new roads or railroads as much as the North did because the South had good waterways on which to ship farm products to market. As a result, the South did not want the government to spend more money improving transportation mainly in the North. *Disagreements over tariffs:* The North wanted tariffs, or taxes, placed on European goods sold in the United States. The South did not want these tariffs. The North's many factory owners wanted protection against cheaper products bought from Europe that would compete with United States products, which were mainly made in the North. In the South, where there were few factories, southerners wanted to buy goods from whoever sold them cheaper—northern or European manufacturers. Southerners thought tariffs would place an unfair advantage on goods made in the United States and higher prices on European goods. *Disagreements over slavery:* All the states in the North had abolished slavery, but slavery still existed in the South. Many northern abolitionists wanted to end slavery entirely. Most southerners did not. The owners of large southern plantations depended on slave labor to grow their crops. Other answers that the students can reasonably support should also be accepted.

   c. Many southern planters thought the end of slavery would ruin them because they depended on slave labor to work their plantations.

3. Congress worked out several compromises to admit new states as free or slave states. These actions kept the balance between the free states that made up the North and the slave states that made up the South. The compromises also gave neither the North nor the South an advantage in Congress and averted any forceful actions from either side for a while. Other answers that the students can reasonably support should also be accepted.

Checking Up (page 223)

1. A system by which people who were against slavery secretly helped slaves escape to freedom in the North.

2. In the North.

3. In the South free blacks had to carry papers with them at all times to prove that they were not runaway slaves. They were also prevented from taking some jobs, yet they could be arrested for not having a job. Some free blacks could even be sold back into slavery. In the North some states did not allow free blacks to vote.

4. a. Successful plantation owners made huge profits, lived in comfortable homes, and held the most power in the South. Small farmers worked hard alongside their few slaves, lived in modest houses or log cabins, and dreamed of being plantation owners someday. Slaves worked hard their whole lives, had very few days of rest, and were often separated from their families. They were told when to work, where to work, and how to work. And very few slaves ever managed to become free. Other answers that the students can reasonably support should also be accepted.

b. Slaves worked in the fields; took care of the farm animals; worked as blacksmiths, carpenters, or other skilled workers; or worked as servants in the planter's home.

c. Many escaped from their owners and traveled to the North, where they would be free. Others organized slave rebellions to march north to freedom.

5. Students might suggest that no person should have the right to own another human being. Slaves were bought and sold as though they were no more than pieces of property. Students might suggest that no person should have the right to treat people as inferiors and subject them to hard labor, punishment, and separation from their families. Other answers that the students can reasonably support should also be accepted.

Checking Up (page 228)

1. Because of his stand against slavery.

2. The Union victory at Gettysburg diminished Lee's hope of convincing the North to end the war. The Union victory at Vicksburg gave the North control of the entire Mississippi River and split the Confederacy in half.

3. a. The election of Abraham Lincoln as president, the secession of eleven southern states, the formation of the Confederate States of America, and the Confederate seizure of United States army forts and weapons in the South, especially the capture of Fort Sumter.

b. The North had more people, more factories to produce weapons and supplies for its army, and more roads and railroads to move troops and equipment. The South needed only to protect its territory from northern armies and had the military advantage of fighting on familiar, southern territory. Other answers that the students can reasonably support should also be accepted.

c. By invading the South and eventually forcing it to surrender. The North won crucial victories in the South along the Mississippi River. As a result, the Union army won control of the entire Mississippi River, which split the Confederacy in half. About the same time, a Union army won an important victory at Gettysburg, forcing Lee to pull back his troops to southern soil. The North's naval blockade of southern ports cut off supplies to the South. To bring the war to an end, the North launched a number of destructive attacks across the South. Finally, Lee surrendered to Grant in April 1865. Other answers that the students can reasonably support should also be accepted.

4. Because Lincoln believed that the Constitution did not give any state the right to secede from the Union. Other answers that the students can reasonably support should also be accepted.

Checking Up (page 233)

1. By this system, poor blacks and whites farmed pieces of land that belonged to the former plantation owners. For the use of the land, the sharecroppers paid the landowners with a share of the crops they grew.

2. The Thirteenth Amendment ended slavery. The Fourteenth Amendment stated that all people in the United States had the same rights. The Fifteenth Amendment gave freed slaves the right to vote.

3. a. A time of rebuilding and reuniting the United States after the Civil War.

b. Freed slaves in the South owned no property, had little or no money to start farms or businesses, could not find jobs, and had little or no education. Other answers that the students can reasonably support should also be accepted.

c. The Freedmen's Bureau provided food for the hungry and medical care for the sick. The agency also set up thousands of new lower-level schools and some colleges for freed slaves.

4. While students' answers will differ, students should be encouraged to support their opinions with facts presented in this chapter. For example, one of the biggest problems was convincing both the North and the South to put aside their differences and work together to rebuild the nation. Congress, which then was made up mainly of northerners, chose a harsh plan of allowing southern states back into the Union. Congress decided to divide the former Confederacy into five military zones, station Union troops there, set up new state governments, and prevent former Confederate leaders from serving in government offices. Many southerners resented

Congress's plans for the South but knew that their states would be readmitted to the Union only after certain conditions had been met. So they worked with northerners to readmit the southern states and rebuild the South and the nation, often with a great deal of tension and resentment.

As You Read (page 234)
Use this reading skill.

States admitted between 1865 and 1890 were Nebraska, Colorado, North Dakota, South Dakota, Montana, Washington, Idaho, and Wyoming.

Checking Up (page 237)

1. For many years settlers had crossed but never settled the vast land in the West between the Missouri River and the West Coast. Farmers were not attracted to the area because they believed the area, made up of the Great Plains and the Great Basin separated by the Rocky Mountains, was too dry for good farming or too hard and mountainous to settle. As a result, the land between the Missouri River and the West Coast was the last area in the United States to attract settlers.

2. Ranchers no longer undertook long cattle drives to get their cattle to market because more railroad lines were built closer to ranches. Ranchers built fences around their ranches to keep their cattle from straying. And many ranchers grew hay to feed their herds through the winter instead of feeding their cattle on range grass.

3. a. As prospectors and miners rushed into a new area, towns sprang up quickly to serve them. Some of these mining towns continued to grow as farmers, ranchers, and more business owners moved to the towns.

   b. As new railroads were completed in the West, new cattle trails came into use for ranchers. By the 1880s the area had enough new railroad lines that very few ranchers had to drive their cattle more than a few hundred miles to a railroad.

   c. Cowhands spent most of their time on horseback doing hard, dull jobs. On the long cattle drives, they had to keep the cattle moving and chase after the strays. The rest of the year, they rode up and down the open range making sure that cattle from their ranch did not get mixed up with other ranchers' cattle.

4. While students' answers may differ, students should be encouraged not only to describe the ways cowhands have been portrayed by television and movies but also to think about what realistic details have been left out. For example, many television shows and movies have classified cowhands as either "good guys" or "bad guys." The good guys wear white hats, try to keep law and order in lawless towns, and protect settlers from hostile Indians. The bad guys wear black hats and do anything they want to, especially if it is against the law. However, in reality, there were many sheriffs and judges who helped keep law and order and administer justice. And most Indians fought only to protect the lands that had always been theirs.

Checking Up (page 241)

1. The Indians, who had lived by hunting buffalo for thousands of years, could no longer follow their old way of life after buffalo hunters had killed nearly all the buffalo herds on the plains.

2. Because there were not enough trees on the plains to supply wood for homes.

3. a. Because new settlers arrived and wanted the Indians' homelands for farms, ranches, and towns.

   b. They had been forced to move to and live on reservations.

   c. Finding enough water, farming the dry grasslands, or finding a substitute for wood for homes, buildings, and fences. To have enough water, farmers dug wells and built windmills to pump the well water or collected rainwater in barrels. To farm the dry grasslands, farmers tried new ways of planting crops or of turning over the soil quickly. To build homes and buildings, farmers used sod. To build fences, farmers used barbed wire. Other answers that the students can reasonably support should also be accepted.

4. Because this was the last unoccupied part of the nation to be settled. Some of the problems that had kept farmers from settling this area—the presence of Indians and the dry land—were

no longer there. The Indians had been forced onto reservations. The problem of dry grasslands was solved as farmers tried new ways of finding water and farming crops on the dry land. In addition, the federal government encouraged farmers to settle the Great Plains. The government offered land to any family that would settle on it, build a house, and farm the land. The chance to own farmland in an area that had never been farmed before was an opportunity many farmers could not pass up. Many who would never be able to afford farmland elsewhere or who lived in an area where farmland was not for sale were also willing to settle the Great Plains. Other answers that the students can reasonably support should also be accepted.

Checking Up (page 245)

1. Conestoga wagon and stagecoach.

2. With the beginning of telegraph service from coast to coast, there was no longer any need to wait ten or more days for messages to come by Pony Express.

UNIT 7 REVIEW WORKSHOP (pages 246–247)

What Have You Learned?

1. Disagreements over government spending for transportation, over tariffs, and over slavery.

2. They worked in the fields.

3. By taking the underground railroad.

4. After the Confederate attack on Fort Sumter in South Carolina on April 12, 1861. Four years.

5. They were given the same rights as other people in the United States, including the right to vote. They were given the opportunity to attend schools and colleges. Other answers that the students can reasonably support should also be accepted.

6. The new southern governments worked to undo many of the rights that blacks had gained during Reconstruction. Laws favoring segregation were passed. In other instances, some southerners tried to keep blacks from voting.

7. Miners, cattle ranchers, and farmers.

8. Transportation of people and goods became faster and cheaper, which encouraged the growth of cities and a great population increase in the West. Other answers that the students can reasonably support should also be accepted.

9. They were made to leave their villages and their hunting grounds. They were then forced onto reservations, where they had to live according to the rules of the United States government.

Use Your Reading Skills

Students should be encouraged to find the meanings of these vocabulary words in the chapter in which they appear or in the Glossary at the back of the book before they write their sentences. These words are all introduced in this unit. The words *tariff* and *compromise* are found in the chapter entitled "Differences in the Growing Nation"; the words *secede*, *civil war*, and *civilian* in the chapter entitled "A Divided Nation"; the word *segregation* in the chapter entitled "Rebuilding the Nation"; and the words *prospector* and *lode* in the chapter entitled "Opening the West."

Use Your Map Skills

1. Virginia. Antietam, Bull Run, Chancellorsville, or Petersburg.

2. On plains. It was easier to move troops, cannons, and supplies over plains rather than over mountainous areas.

3. Mobile and Fort Sumter.

4. The Mississippi and Tennessee rivers. Because it was vital to both the North and the South to control the waterways upon which civilian and military goods and troops were transported.

UNIT 8 A MODERN NATION

Checking Up (page 254)

1. The first world's fair held in the United States and held in honor of the nation's 100th birthday. The fair was a showcase for the latest inventions and discoveries of the time.

2. The steel and oil industries.

3. a. U.S. inventors found new ways of doing things. With new technology, factories turned out more and more goods. The ever-expanding

system of railroads sent goods rapidly and inexpensively to most parts of the country. Rich natural resources were developed, especially newly found deposits of iron ore and oil. Other answers that the students can reasonably support should also be accepted.

  b. Any three: the internal-combustion engine, typewriter, barbed wire, telephone, phonograph, incandescent light, elevated electric railroad, gasoline automobile, radio, and X-ray machine.

  c. Because many workers believed that as members of a labor union they would be better able to bargain with business owners for better wages and working conditions.

4. Telephone communication linked the nation, while the automobile made it possible to travel greater distances over shorter periods of time. The light bulb extended the length of every person's working day. These inventions also made life more comfortable for Americans. At first, only the wealthy could afford these new inventions, but soon everyone wanted and needed them. They became necessities of life. And as people demanded these goods, new factories were built, and workers were hired to produce, sell, and service these new goods. Other answers that the students can reasonably support should also be accepted.

As You Read (page 255)
Use this reading skill.

The table on page 256 gives the number of immigrants who arrived in the United States from selected countries in Europe during the years 1866, 1876, 1886, 1896, and 1906. The table on page 259 gives population statistics showing population growth in selected major cities in the United States from 1880 to 1940.

Checking Up (page 259)

1. To enjoy religious freedom, to escape hunger and poverty in their homelands, to improve their lives by working in the growing industries of the United States, or to start farms on the millions of acres of land still available in this country. Other answers that the students can reasonably support should also be accepted.

2. Many were poor, did not speak English, were not educated, or had few job skills. Those who worked in the cities often had to live in crowded, poor sections. Many children had to work. Other answers that the students can reasonably support should also be accepted.

3. a. People were having large families, and more immigrants were coming to the United States during this time than ever before.

  b. Immigrants from southern and eastern Europe began to arrive in greater numbers and settled mainly in cities.

  c. Because increasing numbers of immigrants and farm workers moved to the cities.

4. Problems that an immigrant family might face include understanding the language, adjusting to a new culture and group of people, meeting new friends, finding a job or activities to keep busy, adjusting to the climate, liking the food, or trying not to miss the people, places, and events in the United States that were left behind. Other answers that the students can reasonably support should also be accepted.

Checking Up (page 263)

1. Its location. An urban area is a city and its surrounding towns, while a rural area is one that is away from cities.

2. The great numbers of immigrants who came to the United States and the great migration of people from rural areas to urban areas.

Checking Up (page 268)

1. Laws were passed setting standards for buildings. Playgrounds were built for children. Settlement houses were started to help the poor learn job skills or English. Other answers that the students can reasonably support should also be accepted.

2. The protection of natural resources.

3. An amendment to the Constitution that gave women the right to vote. 1920.

4. a. Overcrowded slums and poorly built tenements were two problems faced by cities.

  b. More schools were built. By 1918 all states had laws requiring children to attend school. More public schools established kindergartens. Many children traveled to larger schools where more subjects were taught. More women and blacks were admitted to colleges. Other answers that the students can reasonably support should also be accepted.

c. He set aside millions of acres of timberland in the West as a national forest preserve. He set up programs to make better use of the country's water supply and started irrigation projects.

5. Trained, educated workers are necessary to manage and work in factories. Thus, an educational system that trains people in technological advances, such as that in the United States, is an aid to industrial growth. Other answers that the students can reasonably support should also be accepted.

As You Read (page 269)
Use this reading skill.

The Presidents who served terms between 1877 and 1945 were Rutherford B. Hayes, James A. Garfield, Chester A. Arthur, Grover Cleveland (two separate terms), Benjamin Harrison, William McKinley, Theodore Roosevelt, William Howard Taft, Woodrow Wilson, Warren G. Harding, Calvin Coolidge, Herbert C. Hoover, Franklin D. Roosevelt, and Harry S. Truman.

Checking Up (page 273)

1. The United States bought Alaska from Russia in 1867. In 1898 Congress voted to annex the Hawaiian Islands.

2. The U.S. armed forces defeated the Spanish forces. Cuba eventually became independent. The United States took over the Spanish islands of Puerto Rico, Guam, and the Philippines.

3. When Germany surrendered to the Allies on November 11, 1918.

4. a. By buying the land, annexing the land, or winning a war in which lands were awarded to the victor.

b. Because the government became interested in finding a shorter route to its new lands in the Pacific that had been gained in the late 1800s.

c. Because the United States as a world leader felt compelled to help settle the war, especially after the Germans continued to attack neutral U.S. ships carrying supplies to Britain and France and neutral passenger ships carrying U.S. citizens.

5. Because the canal shortened the water route from the Atlantic Ocean to the Pacific Ocean, more ships could travel more quickly and cheaply. Thus, more goods could be traded and transported worldwide. Other answers that the students can reasonably support should also be accepted.

Checking Up (page 279)

1. Any three: the automobile, steel, glass, rubber, and oil industries.

2. Because the demand for farm crops was not as great as before. As a consequence, crop prices fell, which then reduced farmers' incomes and forced many of them to lose their farms.

3. a. Because other industries, such as steel, glass, and rubber, were needed to make products used in the manufacture of automobiles. And with more cars in use, more gasoline and oil produced by the oil industry were needed to run cars.

b. People spent less time preparing food and doing housework, traveled farther and faster in their automobiles, moved to suburbs of cities, traveled more by airplane, or were entertained by radio broadcasts or movies. Other answers that the students can reasonably support should also be accepted.

c. Because many businesses and factories failed and millions of people were out of work.

4. These products made life more comfortable and easier for millions of Americans. Radio entertainment and news broadcasts provided knowledge, culture, and fun. New home appliances such as the vacuum cleaner and the washing machine made housework much easier and less time consuming. With less time spent on housework, family members were freed to do other things. Other answers that the students can reasonably support should also be accepted.

UNIT 8 REVIEW WORKSHOP (pages 280–281)

What Have You Learned?

1. The automobile and the airplane. Other an-

swers that the students can reasonably support should also be accepted.

2. Because workers believed that labor unions would be better able to bargain with business owners for better wages and working conditions.

3. People were having large families, and more immigrants were coming to the United States during this time than ever before.

4. Laws were passed to set standards for buildings, to require children to attend school, and to protect Americans from the unclean handling of meat and the unsafe making of food and medicine. Other answers that the students can reasonably support should also be accepted.

5. Alaska, Hawaii, Puerto Rico, Guam, and the Philippines.

6. In the 1920s business and industry prospered. Americans during this time were able to buy and enjoy more goods than ever before. Inventions and improvements in such things as household appliances, automobiles, airplanes, radio, and movies made life easier, more comfortable, and more enjoyable for millions of Americans. Then in the 1930s, many factories and businesses failed. Millions of people lost their jobs and had no idea when they would be able to find other jobs.

Use Your Reading Skills

1. 116,340 people. 796,841 people.
2. Philadelphia. Chicago.
3. New York. New York.
4. 2,893,623 more people.
5. New York.

Use Your Thinking Skills

1. Some students are listening. Others are reading to themselves or playfully watching their classmates.

2. Some items that probably would not be found in today's classroom are the wood-burning stove, the school bell on the teacher's desk, and the wide-planked wooden floor.

3. The students' clothing and shoes do not seem to be as well made as they are today. Unlike most pupils today, some of the boys are wearing short pants. Today's female teachers usually wear shorter dresses.

4. Some possible answers are a public address system, electric clock, central heating, and movie and slide projectors. Other answers that the students can reasonably support should also be accepted.

UNIT 9 THE UNITED STATES TODAY

Checking Up (page 287)

1. Workers in industry, many of them women who had never before worked, produced material for the United States war effort. The entire country rationed food, gasoline, and many other items. People grew "victory gardens" so they would not use food that could be sent overseas. Other answers that the students can reasonably support should also be accepted.

2. Europe, Africa, and Asia.

3. He was the leader of the Allied forces in Europe.

4. a. Germany, Italy, and Japan were the major Axis powers. The United States, Great Britain, the Soviet Union, China, and France were the major Allied powers.

   b. A dictatorship is a form of government in which one person has total power. Mussolini. Hitler.

   c. The precipitating event was the Japanese attack on Pearl Harbor, but the United States had for many years been opposed to the policies of the Axis countries.

5. More than any other war in history, World War II was fought on a global scale. There was fighting on most of the earth's continents, and many of the countries in the world were involved in the war in some way or other. Other answers that the students can reasonably support should also be accepted.

Checking Up (page 290)

1. The United Nations was founded to keep peace among nations.

2. The Communist government owns most of the land, businesses, and industries in the Soviet Union. The people in the Soviet Union are not free to choose their leaders, nor do they have many of the freedoms Americans have.

3. These nations are called developing because they are only beginning to develop technology and industry.

4. a. The United States helped both Allied and Axis countries rebuild after World War II. Our country has also given aid to developing nations and to the United Nations.

   b. The United States, under the Marshall Plan, rebuilt factories, homes, roads, and railroads in Europe. The United States also helped Japan rebuild and helped the Japanese develop a democratic form of government.

   c. The United States and communist governments have totally different views of government; since many communist governments have tried to force the communist system of rule on other countries, the United States has been drawn into conflicts with many communist countries.

5. People in the United States remembered that one of the principal causes of World War II was the suffering that the losers of World War I had endured. People in the United States wanted peace, not revenge. United States leaders believed that helping the defeated countries rebuild was the best way to assure that peace. Other answers that the students can reasonably support should also be accepted.

Checking Up (page 293)

1. A parallel is a line of latitude, or a line used to find locations north or south of the equator.

2. A meridian is a line of longitude, or a line used to find locations east or west of the prime meridian. Lines of meridians, like parallels, are measured by degrees. The prime meridian, which is 0°, is an imaginary line that runs from the North Pole through Greenwich, England.

3. Every place in the world has a specific latitude and longitude. If a person knows these coordinates, he or she can move north or south from the equator and east or west from the prime meridian and find the location in question.

4. Geographers give the latitude and longitude of the center of the country.

Checking Up (page 297)

1. The building of expressways and the enormous increase in the number of automobiles helped the growth of the suburbs.

2. Americans landed on the moon.

3. a. Technology has made both travel and communication faster, thus connecting places and people in terms of time. Technology's impact on entertainment, especially the development of television, has given everyone in the United States a "connection" to the same sources of information and entertainment. Other answers that the students can reasonably support should also be accepted.

   b. Satellites have expanded the distance over which messages can be relayed. Both television and telephones now rely on satellites to relay signals used in transmitting messages and images across the globe almost instantaneously.

   c. Space exploration has led to developments in computers, transportation, and other aspects of technology, and new information about the moon and other planets.

4. Many people have a curiosity about "the unknown" and a desire to overcome the seemingly impossible odds of traveling to other planets. Other answers that the students can reasonably support should also be accepted.

Checking Up (page 301)

1. The Supreme Court ruled in 1954 that segregated schools were against the law.

2. People in the United States live longer than ever before. Other answers that the students can reasonably support should also be accepted.

3. a. The 1954 Supreme Court decision against segregated schools and the passage of the 1964 Civil Rights Act are probably the two most important victories blacks have won in their efforts to achieve equality.

   b. Hispanic Americans, American Indians, Asian Americans, and women.

   c. Americans retain a belief in the freedoms that are a part of our country's heritage.

4. Although there have been enormous changes in the United States, one of the characteristics of our country that has remained constant is the belief in the ideals of freedom. Other answers that the students can reasonably support should also be accepted.

UNIT 9 REVIEW WORKSHOP
(pages 304–305)

What Have You Learned?

1. The Japanese attacked U.S. armed forces at Pearl Harbor in Hawaii.

2. The Marshall Plan was the plan the United States developed for helping countries in Europe rebuild after World War II. The Marshall Plan involved providing money, food, and other materials to help countries rebuild.

3. Most developing nations suffer from both poor agricultural production and a lack of technology. The United States and the United Nations are trying to help these countries improve food production and health conditions and develop technology.

4. In the 1950s.

5. The building of expressways and the mass production of automobiles.

6. 1969.

7. This act of Congress made it illegal to discriminate against anyone on the basis of race, sex, or place of birth.

8. Doctors and scientists have developed inoculations that can prevent diseases. They have also pointed out that proper sanitation is important in disease prevention.

Use Your Reading Skills

1. Century.
2. Decade.
3. Century.
4. Decade.
5. Century.
6. Century.
7. Decade.

Use Your Math Skills

1. *Car:* 1 hour. *Jet:* 6 minutes.
   Car: 10 hours. *Jet:* 1 hour.
2. *Car:* 2 hours. *Jet:* 12 minutes.
   Car: 20 hours. *Jet:* 2 hours.
3. *Car:* 5 hours. *Jet:* 30 minutes.
   Car: 50 hours. *Jet:* 5 hours.
4. *Car:* 8 hours. *Jet:* 48 minutes.
   Car: 32 hours. *Jet:* 3 hours and 12 minutes.

Use Your Map Skills

1. New York City.
2. Interstate 57 and Interstate 55 or Interstate 55 all the way to New Orleans.
3. Interstate 95.
4. One possible route would be to take Interstate 95 to Interstate 64 as far west as Interstate 44. You could then take Interstate 44 to Interstate 40, which goes all the way to Arizona. Finally, a short trip on Interstate 17 would take you into Phoenix. Other answers that the students can reasonably support should also be accepted.

UNIT 10 THE NORTHEAST

As You Read (page 311)
Use this reading skill.

The inset map shows the location of the Northeast within the United States. Measuring from Boston to Buffalo, the Northeast is about 400 miles (644 km) from east to west. Measuring from the northern border of Maine to Washington, D.C., the Northeast is about 750 miles (1,207 km) from north to south.

Checking Up (page 313)

1. The Northeastern Seaboard. The Rugged Interior. Western Pennsylvania and western New York.

2. The Rugged Interior. The Northeastern Seaboard and western Pennsylvania and western New York.

3. The Rugged Interior's climate, unlike the climate of the Northeastern Seaboard, is not moderated by the Atlantic Ocean. In addition, elevations in the Rugged Interior are greater than in either of the other two subregions. These high elevations cause lower temperatures and also help account for the short growing seasons in the Rugged Interior.

Checking Up (page 317)

1. Most of the people live in urban areas along the Northeastern Seaboard.

2. Some cities have lost part of their populations to suburbs. Many of these same cities have also lost people to areas where new factories have opened up.

TE 48

3. Many immigrants first settled along the Northeastern Seaboard. Even today, immigrants flock to the important cities in the area. Also, because the Northeastern Seaboard is a major center of manufacturing and trade, people have moved to the area to take jobs in the many industries and businesses.

Checking Up (page 321)

1. Dairy farming and lumbering.

2. a. Maine, New Hampshire, Vermont, Massachusetts, Rhode Island, Connecticut, New York, New Jersey, Pennsylvania, Delaware, Maryland. (The District of Columbia is also part of the Northeast.)

   b. The Northeastern Seaboard. The Rugged Interior.

   c. Wholesale and retail trade, manufacturing, and government. Other answers that the students can reasonably support should also be accepted.

3. The cities of the Northeastern Seaboard were the first trading centers in our country. Their importance as trade centers today is, in part, a result of this history. In addition, many of these cities have fine harbors. The proximity of the Northeastern Seaboard to Europe makes these cities logical centers for European trade.

UNIT 10 REVIEW WORKSHOP
(pages 324–325)

What Have You Learned?

1. Plains. Mountains and hills. Mountains and hills.

2. People migrated to the cities of the Northeastern Seaboard to find good jobs.

3. People have left some cities to move to suburbs and/or to find jobs in factories that have been built outside the cities.

4. A megalopolis is a large urban area in which many different cities and suburbs have grown together.

5. Farming, quarrying stone, and lumbering. Manufacturing, wholesale and retail trade, and banking and finance.

6. Pittsburgh in western Pennsylvania and Buffalo in western New York.

Use Your Reading Skills

1. New York. 1970–1980.
2. Between 1960 and 1970.
3. Between 1960 and 1970. New York.
4. All six cities declined in population.

Use Your Thinking Skills

A. 1. Good harbors help make cities centers of trade.

2. The coal in western Pennsylvania helped make Pittsburgh a center of steel manufacturing.

3. Buffalo's location on the Great Lakes has helped make it a shipping center as well as a place to process food shipped on the Great Lakes.

B. 1. Population loss in the cities is due in part to the attractions of living in the suburbs or in the Rugged Interior.

2. The growing population in the Rugged Interior is a result of its beauty and of the good transportation throughout our country.

Use Your Map Skills

1. New Hampshire, Massachusetts, Rhode Island, Connecticut, New York, New Jersey, Pennsylvania, Delaware, Maryland, the District of Columbia.

2. New York, Boston, Baltimore.

3. About 170 miles (274 km). About 160 miles (257 km).

4. Harrisburg, Pennsylvania, is about 150 miles (241 km) inland. Other answers that students can reasonably support should also be accepted.

5. About 420 miles (676 km).

UNIT 11 THE GREAT LAKES REGION

As You Read (page 329)
Use this reading skill.

The subheads for the first chapter, "Where Is the Great Lakes Region?" are **The Region, The Land,** and **The Climate.** There are three subheads under **The Climate: Temperatures, Precipitation,** and **Growing Seasons.**

The subheads for the second chapter, "Where

TE 49

Are the People?" are **Where the People Live** (under which is the subhead **The urban and rural population**), **The Southern Great Lakes Region, Population in the Other Parts of the Region, The Population Growth of the Region,** and **Changes in Population.**

The subheads for the final chapter, "What Do the People Do?" are **Making a Living in the Southern Great Lakes Region, Making a Living in the Farmlands, Making a Living in the Ohio River Valley,** and **Making a Living in the Northlands.** There are two subheads under **Making a Living in the Southern Great Lakes Region: A region of manufacturing** and **Other occupations.** There is one subhead under **Making a Living in the Farmlands: Recent changes.**

Checking Up (page 331)

1. The Great Lakes, the Mississippi River, the Ohio River.
2. Northlands, Southern Great Lakes Region, Farmlands, Ohio River Valley.
3. The Northlands has long, hard winters and short, cool summers. Summer and winter temperatures are generally warmer in the other parts of the region. The amount of precipitation varies within the region, but it does not vary to a great degree.

Checking Up (page 334)

1. Chicago, Detroit, Indianapolis.
2. Smaller cities in the region and the Northlands.
3. Urban growth occurred along the southern shores of Lake Michigan and Lake Erie because in the late 1800s large industries developed in this area. The growth of these industries and the jobs they provided attracted many people. As a result, the population of cities in the area increased greatly.

Checking Up (page 338)

1. Corn.
2. a. Illinois, Indiana, Michigan, Ohio, West Virginia, Wisconsin.
   b. The Southern Great Lakes Region is a densely populated area. The other three areas of this region are not nearly as densely populated.
   c. By working in manufacturing, by mining, by farming. Other answers that the students can reasonably support should also be accepted.
3. Geographic advantages, such as a location close to good waterways, aided the growth of manufacturing in the Southern Great Lakes Region. The Great Lakes and the rivers in this area provide an easy way to move raw materials from their sources to the factories in the cities. Also, finished goods can be shipped by water to markets in other parts of the country.

UNIT 11 REVIEW WORKSHOP (pages 340–341)

What Have You Learned?

1. The Great Lakes, the Mississippi River, the Ohio River.
2. The Farmlands is mainly an area of plains, whereas the Northlands has some hilly areas. The Northlands has shorter summers and longer winters than the Farmlands.
3. Because it is a major industrial area where many people find work in the factories and businesses of the region.
4. A good location close to important waterways and access to raw materials along these waterways aided the growth of industries in Chicago and Detroit.
5. In recent years farm machinery has taken over many of the tasks that used to be done by hand. Also, many farmers specialize, or grow one crop, rather than grow a variety of crops.
6. Because many people mine coal in the area or work in factories that make chemicals from coal.

Use Your Reading Skills

1. Indianapolis, Fort Wayne, Gary, Evansville, South Bend. Springfield, Chicago, Rockford, Peoria, Decatur.
2. All the states in the region.
3. Illinois, Indiana, Ohio, West Virginia.
4. Michigan, Ohio, West Virginia, Wisconsin.

Use Your Thinking Skills

1. The farmhouse and different kinds of barns and silos. The barns probably house livestock and

farm equipment. The silos are used to store feed for animals, usually in the form of silage.

2. Beef cattle and dairy cows.

3. Grains.

4. The farmer probably specializes in growing grains because the fields are large and appear to be planted in only a couple of different ways. Other answers that the students can reasonably support should be accepted.

Use Your Map Skills

1. Lakes Superior, Huron, Erie; Lakes Superior, Huron, Michigan.

2. Wisconsin River.

3. Wabash and Ohio rivers.

Use Your Writing Skills

Although student paragraphs will vary, major points that should be brought out in each paragraph are listed below.

1. Between 1880 and 1950, the population of all the cities listed increased greatly. Since 1950 the population in several cities has decreased somewhat.

2. The population growth between 1880 and 1950 was due to the industrial growth in the region. Job opportunities in the factories attracted many people to the region. The population decrease since 1950 is due to people moving to suburbs or more rural areas. Factories have also moved to suburbs and more rural areas.

3. Since 1970 the population of all the cities listed has decreased. Chicago, for example, had a population decrease of 361,885.

UNIT 12 THE MIDWEST PLAINS

Checking Up (page 347)

1. The western part of the Midwest Region has higher elevations than the eastern part.

2. Temperatures within the Midwest Plains vary because the southern states in the region are hundreds of miles farther south than the northernmost states.

3. Temperature and precipitation are two aspects of climate that vary within the Midwest Plains. Temperatures in the southern part of the region are milder than temperatures in the northern part. Precipitation in the eastern part of the region is greater than in the western part.

Checking Up (page 350)

1. In urban areas.

2. St. Louis, Kansas City, and Minneapolis.

3. Rivers provided the most important transportation routes for Americans in the 1800s. Most of the cities on the Midwest Plains were built in the 1800s. Cities depend on good transportation for trade and food, so the settlers built cities on rivers.

Checking Up (page 354)

1. St. Louis, Omaha, Kansas City.

2. a. Minnesota, Iowa, Missouri, Kansas, Nebraska, South Dakota, North Dakota.

b. Population density within the Midwest Plains is greatest in the eastern part of the region. The population density decreases the farther west in the region one goes.

c. Major crops in this region include wheat, corn, and soybeans. Other crops include rye, barley, hay, flaxseed, and potatoes.

UNIT 12 REVIEW WORKSHOP (pages 356–357)

What Have You Learned?

1. The Badlands are areas in the Dakotas where erosion has created spectacular scenery.

2. Precipitation within the Midwest Plains is greatest in the eastern part of the region and decreases the farther west one goes. Temperatures within the region are coolest in the north and become warmer the farther south one goes.

3. The climate of the eastern part of the Midwest Plains is able to support a denser farm and urban population than the climate of the western part. Both St. Louis and Minneapolis, the two largest cities in the region, are in the eastern part.

4. Twin cities are cities that have grown up on both sides of a river.

5. Spring wheat is planted in the spring and harvested in the fall. Winter wheat is planted in the fall and harvested the following spring.

6. Many cities in the Midwest Plains are centers of transportation because so much food is

shipped from this region to the rest of the country. In addition, the location of these cities in the center of the country helps make them important in transportation.

7. The rural population of the Midwest Plains has declined since the 1920s.

Use Your Reading Skills

Large western farm advantages: greater overall yield of crops or livestock; more efficient use of machinery (e.g., a tractor can work a large farm for about the same cost per hour as it can work a small farm); less risk of total failure (if some crops are lost to flooding or disease, there is still other land that might produce good crops).

Small eastern farm advantages: smaller initial investment; less money spent on fertilizer and irrigation or wells; easier to manage simply because there is less to manage. Other ideas that the students can reasonably support should also be accepted.

Use Your Research Skills

Minnesota—an Indian name meaning "clear water." Iowa—the name of an Indian tribe. Missouri—a French-Indian name meaning "those who have canoes." Kansas—the name of an Indian tribe. Nebraska—an Indian name meaning "flat water." South and North Dakota—the Dakota tribe is also known as the Sioux.

All the names are of Indian origin. One reason the Midwest Plains may have so many Indian place-names is that large, powerful tribes such as the Sioux lived here. Another reason is that this region was settled by people who thought of themselves as Americans and who consequently wanted American names for their states, cities, and towns. The Northeast, on the other hand, was settled by people who considered themselves Europeans—English, French, Dutch—and who wanted European names for their settlements.

Use Your Map Skills

1. North Dakota, Kansas. Kansas.
2. South Dakota. The Black Hills.
3. Coal, lead, silver, iron ore, copper, and zinc. In the southern part of the state.

4. Wichita. Duluth. The mining and processing of these minerals provide important jobs for people in these cities.
5. Iowa, Missouri, North Dakota.

UNIT 13 THE SOUTH

Checking Up (page 363)

1. The Atlantic Ocean, the Mississippi River, the Ohio River.
2. The Gulf Coastal Plain, the Atlantic Coastal Plains.
3. There is a great variety of climates within the South. Florida, for example, has warm, summerlike temperatures most of the year. However, in mountainous areas of the South, temperatures can fall below freezing. Proximity to the ocean also influences the climate of much of the South. Heavy rainfall and even hurricanes are a part of the climate of areas bordering the Gulf of Mexico and the Atlantic Ocean.

Checking Up (page 367)

1. During the 1970s.
2. Workers moving to find jobs with new businesses in the South, retired people. Other answers that the students can reasonably support should also be accepted.
3. The movement of businesses and industry to the South is perhaps the most important factor in this region's population growth. Yet the warm climate is another reason people move here. This region's proximity to Latin America helps explain why there is a growing immigrant population in this region. Other answers that the students can reasonably support should also be accepted.

Checking Up (page 371)

1. There have been recent discoveries of oil and natural gas in and near Louisiana.
2. a. Virginia, North Carolina, South Carolina, Georgia, Florida, Alabama, Tennessee, Kentucky, Arkansas, Mississippi, Louisiana.
   b. Many businesses have moved to the South and have attracted workers to this region. In addition, many minority groups, such as the elderly, blacks, and Cubans, have also moved to

TE 52

the South to take advantage of the boom in jobs and to enjoy the warm climate.

c. Farming, manufacturing, transportation.

3. The high costs of heating will probably force more and more businesses and factories to relocate in the South. Recent discoveries of oil and natural gas will also aid the growth of new industries. Other answers that the students can reasonably support should also be accepted.

UNIT 13 REVIEW WORKSHOP
(pages 374-375)

What Have You Learned?

1. Plains.

2. States in the southern part of this region, like Florida, have growing seasons that last almost the entire year. States in the northern part of this region have shorter growing seasons.

3. The movement of minority groups such as blacks and Cubans into the South is one reason the region's population is growing. Another reason for this region's growth in population is the movement of industries, businesses, and workers into the region.

4. Tobacco, rice, soybeans.

5. Furniture making, textiles, petrochemicals.

6. Atlanta's role as the business capital of the South stems from its importance as the transportation, distribution, and financial center of the South.

Use Your Reading Skills

1. The population of the South is increasing rapidly. (On page 364, the text states that more than 6 million people moved to the South during the 1970s.) The population of the South is changing. (On page 367, the text states that blacks and Cubans are moving into many parts of the South.) The crops important to farmers in the South have changed. (On page 368, the text states that cotton was once "king." Now crops like rice, soybeans, and citrus fruits are vitally important to farmers in the South.)

2. The climate of the South is part of its richness. (On page 363, the growing seasons map shows the long periods of frost-free weather in much of the South.) The South's forests are another source of richness. (On pages 368-369, the text states that forests are an important source of income.) The deposits of oil and natural gas off the coast of Louisiana are another source of richness. (On page 379, the text states that a growing petrochemical industry is using these deposits.)

Use Your Map Skills

1. St. Augustine, Fort Myers.
2. Orlando.
3. Circus Hall of Fame. Busch Gardens.
4. Interstate 4 and U.S. 41.
5. About 75 miles (120 km). About 110 miles (176 km). A little over two hours.

Use Your Math Skills

About 72.7 °F (23 °C).

UNIT 14 THE SOUTHWEST

As You Read (page 379)
Use this reading skill.

The United States acquired most of what is now the Southwest at the end of the Mexican War.

Checking Up (page 380)

1. Some places in the western part of the region have desertlike conditions, while eastern Texas and Oklahoma receive enough rainfall to grow many crops. Temperatures also vary. In high elevations away from the moderating influence of the Gulf of Mexico, temperatures can go well below freezing. In general, though, this region enjoys warm temperatures.

2. The warm winds that blow in from the Gulf of Mexico bring a great deal of rainfall to the eastern part of the Southwest. The gulf also moderates winter temperatures on the Texas coast.

3. Growing seasons within the region vary from north to south, as in all regions of the United States. Generally, the closer an area is to the equator, the longer its growing season. However, in the Southwest the high elevations of some areas shorten growing seasons. The Gulf of Mexico's warm breezes contribute to a long growing season on the Texas coast.

TE 53

Checking Up (page 384)

1. Generally, the most densely populated areas are in the cities of eastern Texas, but there are densely populated areas in each state of this region: around Oklahoma City in Oklahoma, around Albuquerque in New Mexico, and around Phoenix in Arizona.

2. The population of the Southwest's cities increased dramatically.

3. Many parts of the Southwest have a desert-like climate that inhibits development of businesses and housing. In addition, many of these same areas are situated on rugged plateaus or in mountains, which also discourages development. The harsh climate and the landforms of these areas are in contrast to the wet plains of the Gulf Coast.

Checking Up (page 389)

1. Irrigation and deep wells.

2. a. Precipitation patterns vary from east to west. The eastern part of the region receives a great deal more precipitation than the western part. Temperatures within the region generally increase from north to south, but differences in elevation also account for wide differences in temperatures.

   b. For the most part, population density reflects the precipitation patterns. Most of the Southwest's population lives in the eastern part of the region. However, there are areas of high population density in each state of the Southwest.

   c. Natural gas, petroleum, and uranium produced in the Southwest are vital to the rest of the country. There are also many farm products that are grown or raised in the Southwest on which the United States depends: cotton, fruits and vegetables, beef, rice, and sugarcane.

3. One of the most difficult challenges facing this region is supplying people and businesses with water. Another challenge is posed by the rapid growth of the cities. Will these cities continue to offer the advantages that have made them attractive places in which to live and work? Other answers that the students can reasonably support should also be accepted.

UNIT 14 REVIEW WORKSHOP (pages 390–391)

What Have You Learned?

1. Precipitation is greater in the eastern part of the region because it is close to the Gulf of Mexico and the moisture-laden gulf winds. The western part of the region receives dry winds from the deserts of northern Mexico.

2. The Southwest is bordered on the south by Mexico. This accounts for the Mexican influence in the region. The location of many large Indian reservations accounts for the Indian influence in the region.

3. The cities' populations have increased dramatically.

4. The water table is dropping because people have been drilling deep wells to pump water for agriculture, businesses, and human consumption.

5. Oil and natural gas are found in Texas and Oklahoma. Natural gas and uranium are found in New Mexico.

6. Irrigation has made farming possible in many areas of the Southwest that receive very little rainfall.

Use Your Reading Skills

Farms in the eastern part of the Southwest produce a variety of crops. Which crops are grown depends on how close the farm is to the Gulf of Mexico. Close to the gulf, farmers grow crops that need a great deal of rainfall, such as rice. Farther away from the coast, farmers grow crops that do not require so much rainfall, such as corn.

Farms in the western part of the Southwest depend on wells and irrigation to provide water for crops. With this water, farmers can grow crops like cotton or grains. Some farmers and ranchers raise beef cattle.

Use Your Thinking Skills

An increase in the precipitation Phoenix receives would probably have a mixed effect. Farmers near Phoenix would be able to grow a wider variety of crops than they do now. The problems of a dropping water table would probably be relieved because rainfall would begin to replenish underground water supplies. However, the tourist industry and the retirement communities would probably suffer because tourists come to Phoenix to get away from rainy, cloudy weather.

Use Your Math Skills

1. The Navajo Reservation. In New Mexico, Arizona, and Utah.
2. Creek, Cherokee, Choctaw, Osage, and Chickasaw. 84,674.
3. Texas.
4. Four reservations: Papago, Gila River, Fort Apache, and Hopi. 34,202.
5. Three reservations: Southern Pueblo, Zuñi, and San Carlos. 32,325.
6. 305,826.

UNIT 15 THE INTERIOR WEST

As You Read (page 395)

Use this reading skill.

a. An increasing population is the *effect* of people moving to the region to work or to get away from the nation's crowded urban centers. Jobs have been created by the development of the region's natural resources and a growing tourist industry.

b. The recent mining of new natural resources is a *cause* of people moving to the region to work, of the region becoming one of the nation's fastest-growing manufacturing regions, of huge amounts of land being disturbed in the region, and of a new supply of fuels to meet energy needs.

The mining is also an *effect* of new technology being developed to find and process mineral deposits in the region.

c. The growth of manufacturing is the *cause* of people moving to the region to work.

The growth of manufacturing is also the *effect* of the increasing development of the region's natural resources.

Checking Up (page 397)

1. It is the highest land along the Rocky Mountains that separates rivers flowing toward the Atlantic Ocean and rivers flowing toward the Pacific Ocean.

2. Because the Interior West gets so little precipitation, people depend on rivers to supply most of their water needs.

3. All rivers and streams carry some salts that have been washed out of the soil. Usually these salts are carried by rivers out to oceans. In a mountainous area water drains into mountain streams, rivers, or an ocean. In a basin area, however, rivers cannot flow out into an ocean because basin areas are surrounded by higher lands. So the rivers form lakes in the deepest parts of basins. As a result, all the salts that rivers are carrying are deposited into the lakes. As water evaporates from these lakes, they become saltier.

Checking Up (page 400)

1. Denver, Salt Lake City.

2. People are moving to this region to work in jobs created by the development of the region's natural resources, to work in the growing tourist industry, or to get away from the nation's crowded urban centers.

3. No, because much of the region's land is too rugged to be settled, an ever-increasing population accompanied by industrial development may strain the existing water supply beyond what the region's rivers can yield, and the urban centers may begin to resemble the crowded urban centers that people moved away from and thus become also undesirable to live in. Other answers that the students can reasonably support should also be accepted.

Checking Up (page 404)

1. Wheat, sugar beets, potatoes.

2. a. Idaho, Montana, Wyoming, Nevada, Utah, Colorado.

   b. Because of the region's rugged land and arid climate.

   c. Farming and ranching, working in the tourist industry, mining and processing minerals.

3. It has brought new industry to the region to mine and process these natural resources, brought people to the region to work in the development of these resources, and created a need for more goods and services to provide for an ever-increasing population.

UNIT 15 REVIEW WORKSHOP
(pages 406–407)

What Have You Learned?

1. Mountains.
2. Because the region receives very little precipitation.
3. Because people are moving there to work in the growing industries of the region or to get away from the nation's crowded urban centers.
4. The Wasatch Mountain range in Utah and the Snake River valley in Idaho.
5. The tourist industry creates jobs and business for local residents. Workers are needed to maintain tourist recreation areas and to provide goods and services for tourists.
6. Oil, natural gas, coal.

Use Your Reading Skills

Students should make outlines in which the chapter titles are listed with roman numerals. The first-level subheads within each chapter are listed with capital letters. The second-level subheads, which are in boldface and run into the paragraph, are listed with numbers. The third-level subheads, which are in italics and run into the paragraph, are listed with lowercase letters.
   I. Where Is the Interior West?
      A. The Region. The Interior West is made up of six states.
      B. The Land. Much of the region's land is rugged.
         1. The mountains. The Rocky Mountains are located in the Interior West.
            a. The Continental Divide. The Continental Divide is the highest land along the Rocky Mountains.
         2. Plateaus and basins. A broad basin with many plateaus and small mountain ranges is located west of the Rocky Mountains.
         3. The plains. A large plains area is located east of the Rocky Mountains.
      C. The Climate. Much of the Interior West has an arid climate.
         1. Temperature. Landforms and location help explain differences in the region's temperature.
         2. Precipitation. The Interior West gets little precipitation.
         3. The growing season. The growing season is shorter in the Interior West than in most other regions of the country.

Other answers that the students can reasonably support should also be accepted.

Use Your Map Skills

1. Montana.
2. Wyoming.
3. Charles Sheldon Antelope Range, Fallon, or Desert Wildlife Range in Nevada; Fish Springs or Bear River in Utah; National Elk Refuge in Wyoming; or Charles M. Russell Wildlife Range in Montana.
4. Idaho.
5. Mountains.

Use Your Writing Skills

Continental Divide: The highest land along the Rocky Mountains that separates rivers flowing toward the Atlantic Ocean and rivers flowing toward the Pacific Ocean.
Arid: Dry.
Technology: Scientific advances in such things as tools, machines, and transportation.
Oil shale: A certain type of rock from which crude oil can be processed. Other answers that the students can reasonably support should also be accepted.

UNIT 16 THE PACIFIC COAST

As You Read (page 411)
Use this reading skill.

The purpose of the first paragraph is to introduce, in general terms, the Pacific Coast region and to acquaint the reader with those things that make this region distinctive. The purpose of the second paragraph is to locate the Pacific Coast region within the United States as well as within North America. The purpose of the third paragraph is to direct readers to discover how far the

TE 56

region stretches from north to south and from east to west.

Checking Up (page 413)

1. The Sierra Nevada and the Cascades.
2. Along the San Andreas Fault.
3. There are many reasons for the variety of climates within the region. One major factor is the size of the region; from the southern tip of California to northern Washington is a distance of many hundreds of miles. The great variety of landforms is another major factor for the variety of climates. The mountain ranges in this region cool temperatures in some places, cause precipitation to fall in some areas, and shorten growing seasons. The proximity of the Pacific Ocean to this region is a third major factor in creating a variety of climates; the Pacific both inhibits and causes precipitation in different parts of the region. Other answers that the students can reasonably support should also be accepted.

Checking Up (page 416)

1. Southern California.
2. The area between Los Angeles and San Diego is becoming a megalopolis.
3. Many people within the United States will probably migrate to this region to find better jobs and to enjoy the beauty of the region. In addition, the migration of people from other countries will also most likely continue for the same reasons.

Checking Up (page 421)

1. Agriculture, transportation, and entertainment. Other answers that the students can reasonably support should also be accepted.
2. a. The climate varies more from west to east than from north to south. Most of the region bordering the Pacific Ocean has a mild, rainy climate. (Southern California is an exception; this area has a warm, dry climate.) In the eastern part of the region, tall mountain ranges block off the moist ocean breezes. As a result, some of the driest places in the United States are in this region. Although temperatures in the region are generally mild, there can be freezing temperatures in the higher elevations.

   b. Southern California has the highest population density of any area in the region, but urban areas in northern California, Oregon, and Washington also have high population density.

   c. Agricultural products, transportation equipment, and wood products are among the products shipped to other parts of the country. Other answers that the students can reasonably support should also be accepted.
3. The Pacific Ocean affects the region's economy in very direct ways; it enables fishing and tourism to flourish. However, the water that the Pacific provides in the form of precipitation is essential to the agriculture and manufacturing of the region.

UNIT 16 REVIEW WORKSHOP (pages 422–423)

What Have You Learned?

1. Mountains.
2. Areas along the Pacific Coast receive the most rainfall. However, the coastal areas around Los Angeles and San Diego receive very little rainfall.
3. Southern California. Water is brought to this area in aqueducts from waterways many miles away.
4. Southern California.
5. Many different cultures have influenced the architecture, language, and traditions of California, but Mexican and Asian influences have been particularly strong.
6. California (particularly southern California) has a sunny, dry climate. Both the transportation and the movie industries came here originally because they involve outside work, and clear, sunny conditions make such work easier.
7. The Columbia River provides hydroelectric power to both Oregon and Washington. It is also an important transportation route.

Use Your Reading Skills

A microscope is a tool for looking at small things. A micrometer measures extremely small distances. A microclimate is the climate of a small area. A microphone is a device that makes a small sound loud.

Use Your Map Skills

1. The United States and Canada. Washington, Oregon, Idaho, Montana, Utah, Nevada, and part of Wyoming.
2. Seattle and Tacoma.
3. Grand Coulee Dam.
4. Bonneville Dam.
5. Snake River, Willamette River. Astoria, Oregon.

Use Your Thinking Skills

Mountains: Sierra Nevada, the Cascades, the Blue Mountains, and the Coast Ranges.
Deserts: Mojave Desert in southern California.
Valleys: Central Valley in California, Imperial Valley in California, Willamette Valley in Oregon.
Plateaus: Columbia Plateau in eastern Washington.

UNIT 17 ALASKA AND HAWAII

As You Read (page 427)
Use this reading skill.
1959. Juneau. Honolulu.

Checking Up (page 428)

1. A cold, treeless plain.
2. They were formed when volcanoes erupted in the past. The islands are the tops of volcanoes.
3. Climate does vary within Alaska. For example, the Anchorage climatograph tells you that the Anchorage area has a somewhat moderate climate. The average monthly temperatures there do not fall below zero, and in the summer they reach a comfortably cool range. In addition, the *Facts About Alaska and Hawaii* chart tells you that some crops are grown in Alaska. Crops could not be grown in Alaska if the entire state was a cold, arctic region. Other answers that the students can reasonably support should also be accepted.

Checking Up (page 430)

1. In each state's largest city.
2. A group of people who share the same ancestry, customs, and language.
3. The Eskimos, American Indians, and Aleuts. The Polynesians.
4. Much of the state is too mountainous or too cold to settle. Also, Anchorage is well located on a harbor in the southern part of Alaska where the climate is more moderate. Other answers that the students can reasonably support should also be accepted.

Checking Up (page 433)

1. Sugarcane and pineapples.
2. a. Both states are separated from the other forty-eight states.
    b. Because people are moving to each state to fill jobs created by its growing economy. Alaska's growth is due to new discoveries of natural resources. Hawaii's growth is due to a thriving tourist industry.
    c. Working for the military, working in the tourist industry, and farming. Other answers that the students can reasonably support should also be accepted.
3. Because each state's economy is dependent on good transportation to keep the flow of food and other goods going into each state moving, and on the government to keep people employed, especially in military jobs.

UNIT 17 REVIEW WORKSHOP (pages 434–435)

What Have You Learned?

1. Arctic Slope, central Alaska, southern Alaska.
2. Temperatures are warm the year round. They average between 70 °F and 81 °F. There is more precipitation in the winter than in the summer. In the summer months, precipitation averages less than one inch.
3. Most of Alaska's and Hawaii's populations live in each state's largest city.
4. *Alaska:* Eskimos, American Indians, and Aleuts. *Hawaii:* Polynesians and people of European, Japanese, Chinese, and Filipino descent.
5. In both states' economies, transportation and the federal government play major roles. Also, both states must import most of their food as well as other goods.

6. Oil, lumber, fish, furs, gold, tin, or coal. Other answers that the students can reasonably support should also be accepted.

7. Tourism.

Use Your Reading Skills

Land Similarities: Both states are separated from the other forty-eight states. Both are known for the beauty of their landscapes. Both have mountains, hills, and plains.

Land Differences: Alaska is part of a continent, while Hawaii is a group of islands separated from the mainland. Hawaii has volcanoes, while Alaska does not.

Climate Similarity: Both climates are determined by their location.

Climate Differences: Hawaii's climate is warm the year round, while Alaska's climate is moderate to cold. Precipitation is greater in Hawaii than in Alaska.

Population Similarities: Many of the people live in each state's largest city. Most of the rest of each state has few people. In the past twenty years, each state's population has grown considerably. Both states have a variety of ethnic groups.

Population Differences: Alaska's population growth is due to new discoveries of natural resources, while Hawaii's growth is due to a thriving tourist industry.

Economic Similarities: People in both states must import much of their food and other goods. People in both states depend on good transportation to get much of their food and other goods. The cost of living in both states is higher than in many other areas of the United States. Both states are good stopping points for planes and ships, which refuel and take on supplies. In both states many people work for the military to protect our nation's defense.

Economic Differences: Alaska has many natural resources, while Hawaii does not. Tourism is Hawaii's major industry, while in Alaska tourism is not as important. Specialty crops are grown in Hawaii, while there is only some general farming in Alaska. Other answers that the students can reasonably support should also be accepted.

Use Your Math Skills

1. Earlier.
2. Five hours.
3. 6 P.M. 4 P.M. 1 P.M.
4. 11 A.M.

Use Your Thinking Skills

1. Tundra. All have something to do with volcanoes.
2. Hilo. All are cities in Alaska.
3. Aleut. All are ethnic groups that settled in Hawaii.

UNIT 18 CANADA

Checking Up (page 441)

1. There are ten provinces and two territories.
2. Pacific Mountain and Valley Region, Intermountain Region, Rocky Mountains, Interior Plains, Canadian Shield, St. Lawrence Valley, and Appalachian Highlands.
3. Canada's northern location means that temperatures are generally cool and often cold; this aspect of Canada's climate has limited the growth of its population. The rugged landforms in much of the country have also limited the population growth.

Checking Up (page 444)

1. Most of Canada's population lives within 200 miles (320 km) of the United States.
2. Canada's population is much smaller than that of the United States (about 25 million people in Canada, compared with about 227 million people in the United States).
3. Accept answers that the students can reasonably support. You might wish to discuss the benefits of a multicultural society versus the problems of a bilingual society.

Checking Up (page 448)

1. The southern part of the Prairie Provinces and the St. Lawrence Valley in the provinces of Ontario and Quebec.
2. a. Canada shares many of the same landforms and landscapes with the United States: a Pacific Coast area, the Rocky Mountains, an in-

termountain area, an enormous area of plains in the middle of the country, and the Appalachian Highlands. Actually, the countries' main differences are due to location rather than landforms. The United States extends much farther south than Canada, and Canada has a larger part of its territory in the high latitudes than the United States does.

    b. Canada's northern location, generally cool climate, and rugged landforms have limited the growth of its population.

    c. Agriculture, manufacturing (steel and automobiles), and mining. Other answers that the students can reasonably support should also be accepted.

3. Canadians want to have as many different sources of trade as they can. Countries try to avoid relying on only one or two items for trade as much as possible; if prices for the one or two trade items were to fall, a country's economy could suffer greatly.

UNIT 18 REVIEW WORKSHOP (pages 450–451)

What Have You Learned?

1. British Columbia, Alberta, Saskatchewan, Manitoba, Ontario, Quebec, New Brunswick, Prince Edward Island, Newfoundland, and Nova Scotia. Northwest Territories and Yukon Territory.

2. Pacific Mountain and Valley Region, Intermountain Region, Rocky Mountains, Interior Plains, Canadian Shield, St. Lawrence Valley, and Appalachian Highlands.

3. Growing seasons in Canada vary from 7–9 months in southwestern British Columbia to little or no growing season in the northernmost part of the country.

4. Most of Canada's people live close to the United States in the southernmost part of the country. It is in this area, where the climate is mildest and landforms least forbidding, that population is greatest.

5. French and British.

6. Steelmaking, automobiles, paper and wood processing. Other answers that the students can reasonably support should also be accepted.

Use Your Map Skills

1. The northernmost part of the country.

2. The wheat-growing areas in both the United States and Canada are in two rainfall "areas": one area gets 10–20 inches of rainfall each year, and the other gets 20–40 inches each year.

3. Livestock farming areas get the least rainfall. General farming areas get the most rainfall.

4. Rainfall is greatest in both countries in the eastern half and along the Pacific Coast. The Rocky Mountains, which are in both the United States and Canada, prevent moisture-laden winds from reaching the middle of both Canada and the United States.

5. Canada's northern location is the principal reason that there is so much nonagricultural land.

Use Your Thinking Skills

1. Canada's northern location and immense size are two of its most obvious geographic distinctions.

2. Canada's population is centered in the mildest, southernmost part of the country.

3. Canada's economy is based on agriculture, manufacturing, and services. Other ideas should be accepted if the students can support the ideas with facts in the text.

UNIT 19 LATIN AMERICA

As You Read (page 455)
Use this reading skill.

Most of Latin America lies within the low latitudes, or the tropics. Have students look at the climatographs of Belém, Brazil, and Quito, Ecuador, to learn about the climate of locations within the low latitudes.

Checking Up (page 458)

1. Latin America's European settlers came, for the most part, from Spain and Portugal. The languages of these two countries developed from Latin. Because Portuguese and Spanish influence is so strong in this region, it is most often called Latin America.

2. The low latitudes are the region of the world that lies between the Tropic of Cancer and

the Tropic of Capricorn. The low latitudes are also called the tropics.

3. The oceans affect the climates of South America in two very different ways. In much of South America, like Belém, the ocean keeps temperatures warm, and its warm, moist winds provide abundant rainfall. However, on much of the western coast of South America, cold ocean currents make it nearly impossible for precipitation to occur. The cold winds that blow in from the Pacific Ocean prevent warm air from rising and releasing moisture.

Checking Up (page 461)

1. The population of Latin America is growing rapidly and shifting from rural to urban areas.

2. Spanish is the most common language in Latin America.

3. In addition to Spain and Portugal, many European countries had colonies in Latin America during the 1700s and 1800s. In the Caribbean area alone, Great Britain, France, and Holland had colonies. The languages of these colonizing countries can still be heard today on Jamaica (English), Haiti (French), and the Netherlands Antilles (Dutch).

Checking Up (page 465)

1. Coffee, sugarcane, and bananas are three of the most important crops in the tropical regions of Latin America.

2. a. The northernmost part of Latin America (northern Mexico) has landforms and landscapes similar to those of the Southwest region of the United States. Some of Latin America's southern areas (parts of Argentina) resemble the Midwest Plains region of the United States. Yet Latin America's geography differs from that of the United States in one extremely important way. Most of Latin America lies within the low latitudes; most of the United States lies within the middle latitudes.

b. The location of Latin America within the low latitudes is an extremely important fact of its geography; this location affects the climate of the region, which in turn affects its population patterns. In Latin America most of the population lives near the seacoast instead of in the hot, steamy interior. The exceptions to this generalization occur in western South America, where most of the people live on cool, inland plateaus, and in Middle America, where most of the people also live in cool, upland areas away from the warmer coastal areas.

c. Agricultural products, minerals, and manufactured products. Other answers that the students can reasonably support should also be accepted.

3. Prices for all items of trade both rise and fall. If a country depends on only one or two items, it can suffer greatly during a period of falling prices for those items. If a country sells many items on the world market, it is less subject to the whims of the markets for one or two items.

UNIT 19 REVIEW WORKSHOP (pages 468–469)

What Have You Learned?

1. The Andes and the Amazon River.
2. Quito has a much higher elevation than Belém does. The high elevation keeps temperatures cool.
3. Mexico City.
4. Portuguese. Spanish.
5. Mexico, Venezuela, and Ecuador.

Use Your Reading Skills

1. The Atacama is in Peru and northern Chile on the Pacific coast.
2. The winds are chilled because they blow in over a cold ocean current.
3. Warm air must rise and cool.
4. The cold air that comes in off the ocean prevents the warm air near the surface from rising and releasing moisture.

Use Your Map Skills

1. Much of both Middle America and South America has "the longest" growing season because most of the region is located within or close to the low latitudes. The shortest growing seasons are in the Andes, where high elevations are responsible for the short growing season, and at the southern tip of South America, which is close to the polar region of the Southern Hemisphere.

2. All year long.

3. Argentina, Brazil, Paraguay, Bolivia, Colombia, and Venezuela. The growing season is all year long in Colombia, Venezuela, and parts of Brazil. In Argentina, Paraguay, and Bolivia, the growing season is between 9 and 12 months. In southern Argentina, the growing season varies from 5 to 9 months.

4. All year long. These crops are called tropical because they can be grown only in the tropics, or low latitudes.

Use Your Math Skills

1. $30.
2. $1.50. 30 Mexican pesos.
3. $3.50.
4. 4,960 Colombian pesos. $124.

UNIT 20 THE UNITED STATES IN THE 21st CENTURY

Checking Up (page 475)

1. A person who studies population changes or trends to make predictions about future populations.

2. A continued decline in the populations of the Great Lakes Region and the Northeast; an increase in the populations of states in the southern and western parts of the country; the movement of people from urban to rural areas. Other answers that the students can reasonably support should also be accepted.

3. The United States has always been known for welcoming immigrants. This nation was begun by immigrants from Europe. Many of those first settlers and later immigrants came here because they believed that this country was a land of opportunity, equality, and freedom. As the immigration graphs in this chapter show, this tradition continues. Other answers that the students can reasonably support should also be accepted.

Checking Up (page 479)

1. Wind power, solar power, waterpower, or geothermal power.

2. a. There will be greater numbers of people over the age of sixty-five, and more people will be living in the southern and western parts of the country at the beginning of the 21st century than were there at the beginning of the 20th century.

b. Energy resources are needed to run homes, factories, and schools. Yet this nation is faced with a dwindling supply of most of the nonrenewable energy sources now used—oil, natural gas, and coal. Americans are finding it necessary to begin finding and using alternative renewable energy sources so they can be assured of energy supplies in the future.

c. Technological advances may change the way people send and receive information and the type of jobs people will have. Other answers that the students can reasonably support should also be accepted.

3. Americans know that they will need to find new energy sources and adjust to technological advances. Americans have always prided themselves on doing what is needed to preserve this nation for future generations. Other answers that the students can reasonably support should also be accepted.

UNIT 20 REVIEW WORKSHOP (pages 480–481)

What Have You Learned?

1. The southern and western parts of the country.

2. More blacks have been moving to the South than leaving it.

3. Soon after the beginning of the 21st century, all people born during the "baby boom" of 1947–1964 will be in their sixties and seventies. More people were born during the "baby boom" than in comparable periods before or after that time.

4. They can conserve their energy sources more, learn how to design and use more-efficient energy users such as power plants and buildings, or learn how to develop and use alternative renewable energy sources such as wind power and solar power. Other answers that the students can reasonably support should also be accepted.

5. These advances may change the way many people send and receive information, the nature

of jobs, or the working habits of people. Other answers that the students can reasonably support should also be accepted.

6. Because this is the only environment that most future Americans will live in. In order to give those future Americans the same quality environment that is now enjoyed, Americans will need to work on the problems of available energy sources, pollution, and conservation of natural resources. Other answers that the students can reasonably support should also be accepted.

Use Your Reading Skills

1. Wood. Wood.
2. About 1950.
3. 1980.
4. Coal.
5. Because the U.S. will probably rely on "other" sources of energy as our access to supplies of nonrenewable energy sources such as oil, natural gas, and coal continues to diminish. Other answers that the students can reasonably support should also be accepted.

Use Your Map Skills

1. New York and Rhode Island. The Northeast.
2. Washington, D.C., lost 16 percent of its population.
3. Alaska, Nevada, Idaho, Utah, Arizona, Colorado, Wyoming, and Florida. Alaska and Hawaii, Interior West, Southwest, and South.
4. Alaska and Hawaii, Pacific Coast, Interior West, Southwest, and South. Population growth probably will continue because the present population growth trends are so strong in these areas today. Other answers that the students can reasonably support should also be accepted.

Use Your Thinking Skills

Answers that the students can reasonably support should be accepted. Students should be encouraged to give concrete examples of conservation rather than hypothetical ones. For example, students might suggest that their families turn down the thermostat during sleeping hours in the winter.

TEACHER'S NOTES